Praying the Lord's Prayer with Mary

An Imaginative Meditation
by
Susan Muto

With Original Prayer-Poems
by Adrian van Kaam

Resurrection Press
An Imprint of
CATHOLIC BOOK PUBLISHING CO.
Totowa • New Jersey

Imprimatur: Most Reverend Donald William Wuerl
Bishop of Pittsburgh

Nihil Obstat: Joseph J. Kleppner, S.T.L., Ph.D.
Censor Liborum

The Nihil Obstat and the Imprimatur are declarations that this work is considered to be free from doctrinal or moral error. It is not implied that those who have granted the same agree with the contents, opinions, or statements expressed.

Scripture selections are taken from the *New Revised Standard Version.* Catholic Edition. New York: Oxford University Press, 1999.

Excerpts reprinted from *The Book of Concord,* edited by T. G. Tappert, © 1959 by Fortress Press. Used by permission of Augsburg Fortress.

First Published in September, 2001 by
Catholic Book Publishing/Resurrection Press
77 West End Road
Totowa, NJ 07512

© 2001 by the Epiphany Association

ISBN 1-878718-67-3

Library of Congress Catalog Card Number: 2001132757

Cover design and photo by John Murello

Printed in Canada

1 2 3 4 5 6 7 8 9

ACKNOWLEDGMENTS

FOR the inspiration to write this book, we thank Our Lady of Epiphany to whom we have prayed every step of the way.

For the privilege of sharing it with our readers, we thank the staff of the Epiphany Association and, most especially, for tireless dedication in typing and retyping the manuscript, Vicki Bittner; for help with its final presentation, Janice Weaver; and for supervising its production, Mary Lou Perez.

Last, but not least, for their faithful support of our writing and teaching efforts, we express deep gratitude to the members of our Board of Directors and to all our Epiphany Associates. Thanks to their encouragement, we have been blessed by God to give birth to a book we believe will both inspire and challenge you to mature in the life of prayer and to pray the Our Father in a whole new way.

The Lord's Prayer for Shared Prayer

RECOGNIZING that where two or three gather in his name, Jesus, the teacher of prayer, is in their midst, two or three people may place their hands on each other's shoulders and, facing one another, repeat after the leader, pausing after each phrase, the following caring and sharing version of The Lord's Prayer.

God is Our Father. We are one in Christ Jesus.
God's name is holy . . . and so is yours.
I want God's kingdom to come into our life and world. Do you want this too?
May God's will be done among us, everyday of our lives.
Then earth shall mirror heaven.
May God give you daily bread, the bread of life, food for body and soul.
May God forgive all your sins and may you have the grace to forgive those who have sinned against you.
May the Most High God in the name of Jesus and through the power of the Holy Spirit deliver you from evil.
For the kingdom and the power and the glory are God's to give. Receive them, O favored child! Both now and forever. Amen!

Let us now greet one another with a sign of God's peace.

CONTENTS

Mary Remembers

All the prayers of Holy Scripture are summarized in the Lord's
Prayer, and are contained in its immeasurable breadth.
—Dietrich Bonhoeffer

MANY years have passed since that bright, warm day,
etched in a mother's memory, when my Son taught us
how to pray. His words brought as much peace to my heart as
his wounds would one day cause me pain. I am old now, welcoming these times of the day when I can sit bathed in sun-
light, aware of the warmth and glow of his presence.

It seems as if my Son is nearer to me now than when he and
I and our dear Joseph shared our little house in Nazareth.
Soon enough the time would come when crowds of people
would sit in eager circles at his feet, asking him all manner of
things. Young as he was, they recognized my Son as a wise and
learned teacher. I watched as people flocked to him for physical and spiritual healing. It was poignant for me to remember
what happened that day at Cana in Galilee when I told him,
rather matter-of-factly, "They have no wine" [John 2:3].
Everyone who tasted the vintage he blessed still tells of its rare
bouquet and robust flavor. What a miracle that was!

From the moment my child could walk and talk, he always
put others' needs first. He was both solitary and outgoing.

7

Once, when he was twelve and we went to Jerusalem for the Passover festival [see Luke 2:41-45], we almost lost him. A mother's intuition should have told me he would end up with the elders in the temple [see Luke 2:46-47]. I sensed that he wanted to stay there, so inspired were his listeners. Such wisdom in one so young had no precedent. Through the assembly of learned ones, our eyes met. The mixture of sadness and amazement he saw in mine almost brought tears to his eyes. When we asked him what he was doing and he told us he had to be in his Father's house [see Luke 2:48-50], we did not know if he should stay there or return with us. Out of respect and obedience, he made his choice and came with us to Nazareth. There our lives unfolded day by day in simplicity and obscurity for the next eighteen years.

Jesus worked with Joseph in the shop, becoming so skilled that everyone recognized him as the carpenter's son. People would come to them with broken tools, small household items to be fixed, requests for new tables, chairs, chests. All orders were carefully filled and finely crafted. I knew by the length of time the customers stayed that they also wanted to visit with Jesus.

He was the best listener. It was as if he had all the time in the world. He never hurried someone up or interrupted their train of thought. Many times he would answer their questions indirectly by telling a story. These wonderful parables are still repeated by his disciples. They are passed from person to person like precious gems.

The seeds of these stories sprouted like so much else in Nazareth. Ours was a house of prayer despite the usual growing pains. Jesus was such a special lad! On the one hand, he was a typical teenage boy, running, playing with friends, finding any occasion to go fishing. On the other hand, though young in years, he was old in the wisdom and experience that exuded from him.

The love and understanding we shared were remarkable. So in tune were our spirits that before a word was on my tongue he knew the whole of it [see Psalm 139:4]. Once, when he had to journey to a distant town to purchase some equipment Joseph needed, he said, before I could utter a word, "Don't worry, Mother, I'll bring you that cloth you want as well."

These experiences were not a matter of mind reading. We had minds of our own. So deep was the intimacy between us that, more than a son, Jesus was my best friend. Joseph felt the same way. The Father of us all placed him in our care. There was never a moment when he did not respond in kind, listening to us and caring tenderly for us.

Especially unforgettable was that day when the disciples asked him to teach us to pray. Every word of his reply touched me to the core of my being. It was as if I had prayed each one of them a thousand times already. His teaching was so powerful everyone grew still. The words he said were etched on their hearts. They would never forget them. I, too, pray them everyday with awe and gratitude. He could have given me no better gift than this.

He prayed like a child full of trust and lived as an adult full of wisdom. One thought flowed into the next from a source to which we, in our humanness, had no access.

At moments like this I knew him as my son but also, in the spirit of my ancestors, as the Son of Man, the Suffering Servant. Now, since the descent of the Holy Spirit upon us at Pentecost [see Acts 2:1-4], I also know he is my Risen Lord. All that has happened is more than one aging woman can absorb. Soon enough I shall sit on the throne prepared for me since time began by the Father of lights.

Those allusions Jesus made when we would rest by the fire on long evenings come to mind as my earthly end approaches. He would call me, "Queen of heaven," and tell me not to blush! He would say with quiet conviction, "You will intercede for all the women and men on earth. You will be the most powerful prayer the world has ever known." Then I would answer in words that he loved me to repeat, "Here am I, the servant of the Lord; let it be with me according to your word" [Luke 1:38].

These words of mine were first said with consternation and courage when the angel Gabriel came to me with the announcement of Jesus' birth. They really never left my heart. I hope no one ever hears them as the words of a weakling. It took great strength of will to say them. Now that I see all that was contained in this commitment, I thank God for the graces that placed them on my lips.

As I felt the child growing in my womb, pressing against my heart, waves of wonder would overtake me. Many a time I would gasp for breath, only able to say as I did to my dear cousin Elizabeth, "My soul magnifies the Lord, and my spirit rejoices in God my savior.. . .the Mighty One has done great things for me, and holy is his name" [Luke 1:46-49].

So much was done unto me as the years passed that I had no choice but to take the long view, to remember the covenant, to give witness to many doubters that ours is a God who keeps his promises.

There are no words in a mother's way of talking to describe what I went through when his own, "Be it done unto me," came to pass. My intuition again told me, when he went up to Jerusalem, that the time to meet his destiny had come. What a contrast there was between the joy of that last Passover supper and what happened after that. I knew salvation would come at a price, but how could I know how high it would be?

He loved his friends, and one betrayed him. Poor Judas! May God forgive him. When my Beloved Son forgave his enemies from the Cross, I know Judas was among them. Dear Peter repented. The tears he wept carved chasms on his face.

John was and is a great comfort to me, truly another son, but not even his love nor that of the other women who supported me, could soften the agony I, too, had to undergo.

Mothers who have lost sons would perhaps best understand. I felt every lash that ripped his flesh, every thorn that pierced his sweet brow. The nails driven through his wrists were pounded through mine. It was as if all the nails in our carpentry shop were rolled into one and thrust into him. Only oppressors as cruel and powerful as the Romans could have invented a way of torture and death as horrendous as crucifixion.

Every evil the world ever knew, knows now, or will know gathered into one immense force directed at him. Not from so much as one iota of this dark malice did he flinch. Through it all my Son responded with compassion and forgiveness, even granting the repentant thief next to him entrance to heaven [see Luke 23:42-43]. Our mutual "Be it done" came together into one act of atoning, sacrificial love.

By day's end, I held his bent, bruised, dead body in my arms. Strong as he was in life, he felt like a limp baby bird in death. Each bone, though none was broken, had been stretched to the limit. Blood and water oozed from his pores. The body I had bathed and fed, washed and dressed, fussed over as mothers do so many times when he was young, was now fractured, tormented, inert. This lovely boy whom I had rocked to sleep, singing sweet songs, now lay in my arms like some discarded thing.

Nature herself mourned with us: The thunder clapped, the clouds gathered ominously, darkness fell upon the earth and with it a harsh, stinging rain. All that was left for us to do was to place him in the tomb. I knew at some level that much more was to come. The story of his life was not over yet. For now I wanted only to lay him to rest in a dignified way, in a shroud worthy of the Prince of Peace. Then the stone rolled over the entranceway of the tomb provided by Joseph of Arimethea, and it was finished.

But was it? History changed from that moment on. Jesus died and rose again. The Son of Mary and the Son of God were one and the same person. Fully human, my child was also, always, fully divine. He was the Word become flesh in my womb, the God who dwelt among us. We saw in each other the fullness of grace. When he came to us again in risen glory, he was iridescent, translucent with the love of God. He who came into the world as light was light.

When he ascended to heaven after forty days, he must have sensed that there had evolved in our community a faith that would move mountains. Much to my happy surprise, I suddenly stopped missing him in a natural way because I was with him in every way, every day, supernaturally. His presence pervades my being as I share this part of our story. Each time I say the prayer he taught us, its meaning grows deeper.

HYMNS DIVINE

Lady of Epiphany
renewing heart and soul
with hymns of praise
as my spirit dances
through space,
hymns of divine creations
emitting waves of pristine clarity
resonating in the lit up caves
of recollected hearts.

Touched by the light
of his wounded side
my thoughts become
less stale and trite
like fluffs of dust
pirouetting in the air,
I don't know where,
until he turns my melodies
into his hymns
of holy adoration.

CHAPTER ONE

Salutation

"Our Father"

Anyone with a bit of good sense would not make so bold as to call
God by the name of Father until he had come to be like him.
—Gregory of Nyssa

I WILL never forget the astonishment on the faces of the
people when Jesus greeted the Father in this way. With two
simple words, he dispelled their assumptions that God's name
was too holy even to mention. God was for them utterly
almighty. He was beyond words, images, thoughts, symbols.
He was their Maker.

How we greet a person signifies for us what our bond with
him or her is. That it was right and proper to call this awesome
God of our covenanted heritage not only "Father" but also
"Daddy" (*Abba*) was nothing short of revolutionary.

Jesus, one with the Father yet one of us in all things but sin;
Jesus, my Son and the foster child of Joseph, knew that this
way of greeting God would help us to pray. With two words of
salutation, he introduced our people to God as the One who
hears them. Their heavenly Father cares so much for them that
he knows when even one hair falls from their head [see
Matthew 10:30], for all of them have been counted. Indeed, as

Jesus said, "Are not two sparrows sold for a penny? Yet not one of them will fall to the ground unperceived by your Father" [Matthew 10:29].

These opening words of the Lord's Prayer were like music in our ears. The Father of my Son was the Father of everyone. He is the God of all that is, was, and will be. He is ours and we are his.

When in memory I return to that scene, I can recall people's ears perking up: "What can he be saying? God is God. We humans are mere creatures, here today, gone tomorrow. Does not Scripture tell us that we are like chaff blowing in the wind? He speaks as if we could be drawn into a person-to-Person relationship with the Most High. That is too much to hope for, too much to believe."

As if foreseeing their thoughts, Jesus paused at the end of this salutation, letting his words sink into their hearts. The people waited, wondering what was next. How he prayed was startling to people hungering for some relief from their harsh lives.

If what Jesus said were true, it meant that Jews and Gentiles alike were loved by God. He was not *my* Father or *yours;* he was *our* Father. In his loving eyes, we were all children of God, equal by virtue of our creation, male and female, made in the image and likeness of God [see Genesis 1:26- 27].

This good news would bring an end to the feeling of our having to prove ourselves to God, as if his love were not greater than our mistakes.

Jesus challenged the people on another occasion, asking them: "Is there anyone among you who, if your child asks for bread, will give a stone? Or if the child asks for a fish, will give a snake?" [Matthew 7:9-10].

My Son told many "father" stories, not only because he knew the Father but because he wanted to show the depth of his love and the length to which it would go to save us.

In my own childhood prayers I had intuited this teaching. I was blessed with good, holy parents, Joachim and Anna. They were godfearing people, obedient to the Jewish law, teaching it to me by example as well as word. For reasons I now understand, I could never hold God at arm's length. Every time I opened the Scriptures they spoke to me of his care and concern. I started to pray to him—not so much with formal words as with simple heart-to-heart exchanges.

I talked to God trustingly, as if I were speaking to my own father. Only God knew the secrets of my soul. I brought before him all the strange longings I felt as a young girl. I knew that I was different from others—no less a child and teenager, but one who sensed that some awesome destiny awaited her. I really needed a Father who understood me thoroughly, and he was there. I felt able to address him as only a daughter could.

There was never any question as to the depth of my obedience. He knew that I would remain faithful to his will, not because I did not have a will of my own but because, "Yes, Father," became the words that gave me the greatest joy.

Knowledge of where that "Yes" would lead me was, of course, not yet available to me. I only knew at some level that much would be asked of me. I fully trusted the Father. He would give me the grace to respond according to his will.

When Jesus was born, I and Joseph embraced him as "our" Father's greatest gift. We were three unique creatures but, at the same time, we were one in the Father. Think, then, of the wonder we felt when our Son told us that he and the Father were one [see John 17:21]!

As a mother at home with her child, I saw many signs of their infinite intimacy. This was the gift Jesus passed on to us by his insistence that we address God as "Our Father," the gift of intimacy with God.

Once in a while when, for example, I came quietly into the house to begin meal preparations, I would hear whispers in the next room. At first I thought Jesus was playing with one of his neighborhood friends. Our house was a place where many of the children liked to come. They all wanted to be with Jesus. As I tiptoed toward his room I realized he was not alone. The Person with whom he was conversing was his Father in heaven.

This was one of many moments when my Son, young as he was, became my teacher. The words he spoke were not audible, nor was it my place to try to overhear them. It was enough to behold his rapt attention, the glow of sheer joy on his face, the occasional outburst of happy laughter. The child at prayer then was the man who stood before us now, responding with the affection a good teacher feels for those who are eager to learn.

If they wanted to know how to pray, they had to start with the right greeting, and it was "Our Father." The word Jesus favored, a word John, his beloved disciple so often would use in his writings, was "love." God, the solicitous Creator of every living thing, was love [see 1 John 4:8].

For farmers and slaves, sinners and prostitutes, pharisees and tax collectors, such things were a revelation. One woman came to me with tears in her eyes. She confessed to being without hope. As a poor widow, what was she to do? God had to attend to so many other important things. Why would he care about her plight? How could One so lofty love a person as lowly as she?

As soon as she heard my Son say that it was permissible for her to address God as if he were her own father—not in human terms, because her earthly parents were far from perfect, but in terms of her relationship with God—her whole demeanor changed. She felt the bond of love between her and God tighten, almost like a marriage knot! She experienced a surge of warm affection for her neighbors. They, too, seemed to respond with relaxed countenances to this good news.

Jesus had a way of shrinking the distance between us and God. He brought what was high into consonance with what was low. He was like a bridge between heaven and earth. When he later revealed to his disciples that to see him was to see the Father [see John 14:9-11], it was as if this salutation rose spontaneously to their lips.

There have been many mystical moments in my life, accompanied by all the awe they bring. Once I was lifted in prayer to a high plain of union. There I heard the Father say that "because you are mine, all that I have is yours and all that you have is mine."

This is not a salutation to be glossed over lightly. When Jesus greeted the Father in this way, he paused while the salutation sunk in. Before going further, he took people to a new place of prayer—from distance to nearness, from forgetfulness of God to remembrance of their divine paternity, from feeling like lost sheep to becoming lambs slung over this loving shepherd's shoulders.

In my lifetime, I have seen the best and the worst of the human condition. I have known ecstasy as high as the sky and the fear that paralyzes an immigrant in a foreign land. In my lifetime empires have fallen. New waves of civilization have commenced. Change never ceases. Yet we humans need to rest on a foundation, to find the wellspring, the source, the fountainhead of our existence. This is the Father. When anyone greets him as my Son taught us to do, they stand on the ground of their true identity because the Father is the Divine Mystery from whom all life forms are created and to whom all shall return.

Jesus said to us in those last days that he was going to the Father, to a place where we could not follow. He would go ahead to prepare the way for us. Now, in my older years, as I walk here and there and feel my legs shake a bit, I know I shall soon be with him in his glory.

He who made us, who loves us, who sustains us—he who is love, he to whom I am both daughter and bride, is the Father we greet with this simple salutation. Because we have the same Father, we are, as Jesus taught us, no longer servants but friends [see John 15:15]. We call God by the same name my child so often uttered, the name "Abba" [see Galatians 4:6]. He shelters us in his arms as tenderly as any nursing mother [see Psalm 131:2]. "How do I know this is so?" you ask. "Because I cradled his Son. Because I felt the beat of his heart against mine. Because I am embraced, as you are, by his risen presence."

SALUTATION

Divine salutation of each event,
perpetuating the trend
of transfiguration
of humanity's mystery
with its misery blinding me
to my call to majesty.

Salutation to Mary,
deeper greeting than any creature
ever could receive.

Still recipient,
your sin-free purity
cannot be equaled
by anyone
born under
the burden of the Fall.

O plead with the Spirit,
your lovely groom,
to drive from me
the gloom
dimming the joyousness
of his salutation
of my own small destiny
in space and time.

Mary, I salute your proximity
to the wellspring of generosity.
touched you were
by the wonder of your life rent asunder
by the summons to at-homeness
in the cloister of the Trinity.

Draw me with you into their intimacy,
abyss of infinity
that makes me be.

I am like chaff
blowing in the wind
of whimsical distraction,
silencing the melody
of your Son's invitation
to enter silently his family
adopting me,
O loving bosom of the Trinity.

Looking in your Son's
eyes filled with love
you saw in silent adoration
the many faces of the children
of Our Father to whom
he would bring salvation,
a wounded people of past and present ages,
racing toward millennia to come.
By this holy salutation,
help us to root our faith
in the embrace
that signifies
so lovingly
our longed for destination.

CHAPTER TWO

Destination

"Who Art in Heaven"

To return to heaven there is only one route and that is to admit one's sinfulness and seek to avoid it. To make the decision to avoid it is already to be perfecting one's likeness to God.
—Gregory of Nyssa

I THOUGHT I was alone in our garden that day. As my Son rounded the corner, he seemed to see in an instant, despite my welcome smile, the small furrow of worry on my forehead. He had told me many times not to be anxious or afraid. I trusted him, and I loved him more than words could say. Though I felt at peace inwardly, fully surrendered to the Father, there were times when I felt fretful about my boy's future.

I caught some lines of concern on his brow too. I sensed his pain in the face of humankind's perilous choices. Our shared sensitivity to evil in any form was acute. It brought us, both when we were alone and together, to our knees.

On that day, I remember him coming over to me, taking my face in his hands, looking deeply into my eyes, and saying, "Mother, these troubles will pass away soon enough. You must see them in view of the Father's providential plan. As he has decreed, you shall one day be the Queen of Heaven, forever at my side."

He left me with those solemn words, and I felt the weight of worry lift from my shoulders. Later he would tell those whose life had become too much to bear, "Come to me, all you that are weary and are carrying heavy burdens, and I will give you rest. Take my yoke upon you, and learn from me; for I am gentle and humble in heart, and you will find rest for your souls" [Matthew 11:28- 29].

He prayed, "Who art in heaven," with a slow, steady voice. He spoke of the Father not in the past tense, but in the present. The Father who is, was, and will be, is everywhere at once. He is the same, now and forever. Many thought of God as a distant deity, remote from the created world, indifferent to our plight. We people of the covenant knew better. God was "Emmanuel"—God-with-us. It is in him that we live and move and have our being [see Acts 17:28]. As God himself revealed to his people, "I am who I am" [Exodus 3:14].

Many who heard Jesus' instructions that day had no concept of life after death. Most did not know what to believe would happen once they took their last breath. What was this heaven of which he spoke? Where was it? Was it a place bound by time and space, like a great kingdom hanging somewhere in the cosmos? And, did the Father live there as a ruler in a castle?

Some shook their heads when he said, "Who art in heaven." He did not say, "Who art in the heavens," because that might mean that God was an impersonal force diffused through the universe like air. It was as if Jesus were telling them of a place beyond earthly description, a destination toward which all repentant souls were being led.

I could see that the notion of a heavenly home touched many hearts, and it was not hard to see why. One afternoon Jesus and I were walking together in the environs of Nazareth. As we paused to take in the vista, Jesus said, "What a truly heavenly day this is! May it last into eternity, Mother. May the joy we feel at this moment never end!"

We kept walking, arm in arm, toward the village, chatting about the new orders Joseph had received, expressing the concern we felt for his failing health, singing our gratitude to God for the abundance of this year's harvest.

When we got to the marketplace, the scene was sheer chaos compared to the peace of our journey there. Merchants hawked their wares. Beggars occupied every corner they could find, pleading for a few pennies. We always gave what we had, though our modest means prevented us from giving as much as we would have liked to offer.

Just then Jesus spoke to me with words that stirred to the quick my motherly heart. "They are like sheep without a shepherd" [see Luke 15: 3-7]. I, who have been blessed by God from the beginning with a sense of my life direction, beheld with compassion their seemingly directionless behavior. So many people lived for the moment, buying and selling, eating and sleeping, seeking pleasure and instant gratification as if there were no tomorrow, as if there were no God to whom they would soon enough have to report their doings. How many invitations of grace passed them by because they were too busy to listen to the still, small whispers of the Holy Spirit?

By telling us to pray to our Father in heaven, Jesus gave us a destiny and a destination.

I believe he wanted people to think of their life as a whole when they meditated upon these words. From whence did they come? Where are they now? Where do they hope to be? Nothing pains my Son more than to see the emptiness and desperation in the lives of so many people.

When believers come to accept Jesus as their Savior, as the one who goes before them to prepare the way [see John 16:10], their lives take on meaning and purpose. The length of their days on earth is as a breath compared to the eternity that awaits them in the "many dwelling-places"of Father's house [see John 14:2].

After the resurrection, and especially after Pentecost, many came to believe. Long before he ascended to heaven to sit at the right hand of the Father, people shared the story of how he had changed their lives for the better. One evening, as I sat with the apostles talking about the shape the community of believers seemed to be taking, we asked ourselves why the message found such fertile grounds of fulfillment.

Peter said, "It is because they have come not only to love the Lord and his teaching as we try to hand it on but because his message makes sense from their own experience. Our people know oppression. They believe that there has to be a greater meaning to life than being born, working oneself to death, and going forgotten to the grave. Whether one is buried a pauper in an unmarked cave or a rich man in a marble tomb, the end is the same: no one escapes death's sting" [see 1 Corinthians 15:54-57].

"But Jesus has overcome death. He has given us believers a sense of hope in the face of seeming hopelessness, for nothing is impossible for God [see Matthew 17:20-21]. There is more to life than sheer living and dying. There is life beyond the grave, life eternal! Heaven is our true destination. Even now, thanks to Jesus, we are being invited to the divine banquet table. Knowing our destination gives us a new view of our life as a whole."

We knew from what they told us that this promise gave our people new hope. They could believe in things unseen. They could claim God is their Father. O how we longed to be with him and Jesus and the Holy Spirit and all the holy ones of God forever!

After all, as John reminded me that evening,"Jesus called you the Queen of heaven." How could we doubt what a wondrous destiny he has in store for us!"

I sit now in the sun of Ephesus reminiscent of our old life in Nazareth, awaiting with joy the designated time of my entrance to eternity, aware of the omnipresence of God, of the divine embrace. The promise of heaven lies before me and for all who believe like me, but it is at my doorstep here and now.

I glimpse our destiny when on cool mornings I hear a lark sing or see the dew on desert plants. I am touched by the eternal when I rub the gnarled skin of a ripe orange or taste its sweet fruit and smell its heavenly aroma.

Jesus taught us never to confine the Father to any one word or image, symbol or learned text. The mystery of divinity escapes human grasp. The Father is beyond all and yet, he is in all—as he is in heaven.

That little word *"in"* is important, too. The Father is a person, not a "What," but a Who. He is *in* heaven. For this reason, we are invited to sup at his table *in* eternity, to come to know and adore him *in*wardly, to live and move *in* him. Most of all, Jesus wants us to know the Father *in*timately. That is the reason for our prayer.

The best times Joseph and I spent with our Son, already in Egypt, during our flight there under protection of the angels, and later in Nazareth, were the times of shared prayer. With or without words, we felt between us a growing sense of *in*timacy. We were, as I now dare to say, *in* heaven.

The sad fact is that long before death people seem to choose their destiny. My Son has great compassion for dying sinners and hears the prayers we say for them. So often people could have heaven for the asking, but they choose the hell of a selfish life instead.

That is why to this day I feel such compassion for Judas. He walked with Jesus and the other apostles. He must have experienced in Jesus' presence moments of heavenly bliss. How could he choose a cowardly act of betrayal over the selfless gift of loyalty? I have no reply to this question. All I know is that the Father will not interfere with our free choice. Will it be life or death? Heaven or hell?

"Choose heaven," Jesus seems to say. "My Father is there to welcome you, his sons and daughters. I have gone before you to prepare a place. Become, then, like little children without guile and innocent of sin. Trust that through my mercy you shall enter the kingdom of God [see Luke 18:16-17]. You shall sit at the banquet table we have prepared for you from the beginning of time."

DESTINATION

Woman of sorrows,
sharing your Son's dying,
your heart overflowing
with divine knowing
of your destiny
to share Jesus' bloody banquet
on earth and in eternity.

In Ephesus,
on your street,
you saw people
clutching weeds
of ambition and success
in their fleetingness.

Lost in empty slots
of pleasure and possession
they did not listen quietly
to the whispered melody
of Father's will
in the recesses of their soul.

In our soul there sings the
melancholy tone
of longing for a final home
created in the abyss
of the beginning
orchestrated by your Son
whose blood won
by grace
this everlasting place
that shall be our own.

Rekindle my hope
that the Father
will turn my soul
with Son and Spirit blest,
into a gentle berth
in the midst of the cacophony
of resentment, envy, hostility
that shadows my and your humanity.

O woman, full of grace,
let people no longer hunt
for only money, status, fame
disguising the deeper destination
of goodness, love, and charity
that make them one
in the kingdom
of your Son.

CHAPTER THREE

Adoration

"Hallowed be Thy Name"

Jesus' prayer teaches us that God is holy. It helps us to discover the holiness of the Being that creates, provides, judges, chooses, and abounds in generosity, welcomes and rejects, rewards and punishes equally. This is what characterizes the quality that belongs to God, the quality that the Scriptures call by the name of God. —Origen

WHEN Jesus offered such honor to the Father, he bowed his head and a hush came over the crowd. The silence signified how holy the name of God is in our tradition. The thought of taking God's name in vain or being guilty of blasphemy or swearing by it not only violated the ancient prohibition; it offended any believer who heard it.

Whenever Jesus invoked the Father's name, aloud or to himself, when we shared prayers of adoration or he went off to a quiet place to pray, a sense of awe overtook him. Light seemed to radiate from him. Wonder broke forth in songs of praise.

Jesus loved to walk up into the hills by himself. He knew the name of every bird and wildflower. When he picked a bouquet and brought it to me to place on the table, he would take great delight in either making me guess its name or telling me in glow-ing detail about its history. "Before the world began, he knew the whole of it," I would say to myself. "He is the Word spoken by the Father through whom all that is came to be" [see John 1:1].

When a new baby was born in the village, his or her parents began to ask Jesus, "What should we name our child?" Whether he wanted to or not, he earned a reputation of picking just the right one. It was as if he could see who the child was destined to be and name him or her accordingly.

A name is a mystery. Why Mary? Why Joseph or Elizabeth or John? Yet in our name resides something of who we are. Even Peter would say of Jesus: "You are the Messiah, the Son of the living God" [Matthew 16:16].

Often I pray now with only the name of Jesus on my lips. It says everything to me. I abide for hours in the aura of my Son's name, attentive to all the names, alike in meaning, by which he has come to be known—Prince of Peace, Messiah, Emmanuel. I do so, even though I know that no name can exhaust his mystery.

Had his name been hallowed, the crowd could never have shouted, "Crucify him!" Evil was afoot on that horrendous day. All the reverence and respect due to Jesus as "Son of the Living God," turned to malice. His name was spit out like a glob of venom. Soldiers cursed at him. The crowd swore. I wondered if he did not suffer more from these insults than from the lashes they gave him. His persecutors challenged him to come down from the cross, to call on the angels to defend him. The more silent he became, the more loudly they shouted at him.

The words that tore my heart in two were those he gasped toward the end of his bodily life. It was when he called upon the Father by name, asking why he had abandoned him [see Matthew 27:46]. Oh! The sheer agony of it. Then he commended his spirit into his Father's hands in a gesture of surrender seen as defeat only in the eyes of unbelievers. I watched as the heavens opened to receive him.

In this part of his prayer, Jesus asks us to make a commitment: that the name of God will always be hallowed. Sad to say, the adoration God commands is all too often disavowed and abused.

Even as I share these memories of my life with Jesus, I hear his name taken in scurrilous, blasphemous ways. I can hardly believe it is happening. Every time it does I almost wish I could hold my ears shut. I beg him not to judge the world harshly but to show mercy to his people.

The other day, when I went to the marketplace, I was browsing near a fruit stand. A beggar boy, so emaciated his bones were stretched across his skin, stood looking at the produce, especially the juicy oranges. Inadvertently, he reached for one—not to steal it but to touch it, as if its scent alone would sustain him. The vendor flew into a rage and, not knowing who I was, shouted, "Jesus Christ! You get out of here or I'll tan your hide!"

The boy took off as fast as he could. I stood there dumbfounded. The merchant must have seen the shocked expression on my face because he muttered something under his breath and went back into the shop. I began immediately to pray—for him, for the boy, for anyone, anywhere, who refuses to keep God's name holy, who becomes so indifferent to using it that irreverence is more customary than courtesy.

The crowd listening to Jesus was not without guilt. Violation of the commandment not to take the name of the Lord in vain [see Deuteronomy 5:11] had probably occurred many times already that day. Perhaps that is why so many, who gathered to listen to Jesus teach, looked a little sheepish. Now the master was inviting them to look again at their ways. He was doing so not by preaching a sermon but by asking them to join him in prayer. He believed, as I do, that if hearts hardened by sin learned to hallow the name of God, the reform of their lives would begin. If people do not adore and revere God, how can they learn to respect one another?

As a mother, I tended to want to defend Jesus when he was growing up, although I knew it was important for him to stand up for himself and establish his own good name. Still it hurt me when he and other good boys in the village were the brunt of name-calling. Had he felt defensive rather than forgiving, the abuse would have become worse. He never called others by anything but their true name, even when they made fun of him. His close friends listened and learned, but many resisted such example. He chose to present their names personally to the Father when he prayed. It was as if he were setting them—body and soul—at the foot of God's throne. Even if they did not hallow God's name, he would do it for them.

I believe people understood, as I did, that the first lines of Jesus' prayer, "Our Father, who art in heaven," would remind them of the First Commandment. When we greet God in this way, when we adore his heavenly majesty, we cannot help but obey the Second Commandment. It invites us to hallow God's name, which is to say not to take it in vain.

In these days of revelation, after the resurrection of my Son, when so many want to hear the good news preached to them and to receive baptism, it is best to begin their learning in the name of the Father, and of the Son, and of the Holy Spirit.

The name of Jesus, said with fervor and appreciation, contains within itself all they initially need to know. When inspired by their adoration, people hunger to know more—to grasp the essence of his message. I have seen converts weeping tears of repentance when for the first time they hallow his name as their Messiah. How it softens their heart to know him as their personal Savior and loving God.

The name is the portal through which people come to know my Son more intimately. His prayer is both a reminder of and the reason why they want to enkindle in themselves the fire of conversion.

The crowd, fascinated as they were by his prayer, repeated with reverence, "Hallowed be thy name." It was if they were asking forgiveness for all the times they had insulted God by their less than adoring behavior.

Never will I forget the grace of that moment. People felt the conviction in Jesus' voice. Later they said among themselves: "He gave us, the likes of us—thieves and teachers, beggars and bankers, publicans and physicians—the chance to give glory to God's name. Every time we say this prayer, we taste a bit of heaven."

For whatever reason I'll never forget a day in Jesus' young life, when he was perhaps seven or eight years old. He saw me fretting over a woolen shirt that had shrunk to half its size. He held it up to his chest. We both laughed. It was so small it could hardly fit a three year old. Then he said something wise beyond his years. "Mother, that's what I want to do—not shrink cloth but shrink the distance between people and God."

Jesus told us on more than one occasion that his Father not only loves us but calls us by name. It is only fitting that we honor God's name, but the wonder is that God honors ours. Yet what name can capture all that a person is?

When my kinswoman, Elizabeth, gave birth to her son and, as God willed, called him John, she could not foresee, anymore than I could with Jesus, what power and hope resided in that name [see Luke 1:63]. So known did the Baptizer become as the one sent by God to prepare the way for Jesus [see Luke 3:4] that Herod beheaded him [see Luke 9:9]. But it was too late to stop the far greater fame of Jesus' name from spreading to the four corners of the earth.

John so hallowed the name of God that he went to the desert to penetrate its mystery. Adoration and awe were synonymous with his mission. When he saw Jesus the day he baptized him in the Jordan, he identified him immediately as the One who was to come, God's Anointed, the strap of whose sandal he was not fit to loosen [see Luke 3:16].

The earth bowed low that day. The heavens opened. It was the Father's turn to hallow his Son, whom he called, as the Holy Spirit overshadowed him, "You are my Son, the Beloved; with you I am well pleased" [Luke 3:22].

Never a day went by in our home when we did not pray. We especially loved the psalms. They were as familiar to us as food on the table. What spiritual nourishment they gave us! Jesus loved them all. He knew them, as he knew all of scripture, by heart.

Once, late in the day, he went for a walk with his friends. It was getting dark, and I wondered where he could be. Then I looked out the window. I saw him walking in the lane. He was coming toward the house when suddenly he stopped. There was a space in our small courtyard where one could look above the rooftops and see the stars. I respected his wish not to come into the house just then but to sit on the small bench in our garden until night fell.

He loved the stars and had no trouble naming them. I could tell he was entering into deep contemplation. In my heart I prayed with him. I may have dozed off for a moment, for when I awakened I heard, as with my inner ears, soft voices. I looked out the window, and Jesus was still there. He had risen from the bench and stood upright with his arms raised to heaven. Then he began to dance around the yard in a spirit of joyful, childlike abandonment. In a whisper, as if his words were wired to heaven on the night wind, he prayed, "Holy is your name, O Lord, and holy is the place wherein you dwell."

The refrain lifted me beyond myself into a disposition of pure awe and adoration. I saw for one flashing moment the passing of time, age upon age when the words of the prayer Jesus taught us would be written on the hearts of the multitudes in search of meaning for their lives. There was no other phrase to utter than "Hallowed be Thy Name."

ADORATION

Mary, I watch you
gazing at the pagan city
at your feet.
You see people
awakening in every street,
catching the rays
of sunshine
reflecting the radiance
of Jesus' face,
illumined by the trace
of awe-filled adoration
suffusing his being,
absorbing him in the mystery
of Father's will,
inwardly alert, yet still.

Mother, most kind,
my joyous heart,
leaps up like a flame,
at the sound of his name.
Attune its vibration
to your own adoration.
Beg the Father with Jesus
that all may be touched
by your Son's revelation.

Mother, most mild,
when people do not hallow God's name,
using it in vain,
fill them with shame.
Let them sense in awe
the tear in Jesus' heart,
at any betrayal

of the love of God.
Let them never disavow
the holy name nor allow
their tongue to utter it jokingly,
as a curse or, even worse,
as an expletive of short temper
when things go wrong.

Mother, most strong,
when the throng of daily events
becomes too much for me
to bear with patiently,
let me see
that Jesus suffers silently
when I demean the name,
instead of bowing my head
and bending my knee
in silent adoration,
hallowing its holy sound
beyond and in the round
of daily doings.

Let me embrace with thee
this sacred token of his caring
in any event, as well as in the inner bent
of fickle heart and mind.
Unwind my absorption
in worldly things alone.
Speak my name.
Lead me home.

CHAPTER FOUR

Expectation

"Thy Kingdom Come"

The kingdom will not reach its fullness in each of us until wisdom and the other virtues are perfected in us. Perfection is reached at the end of a journey, so we ought to be 'forgetting what lies behind and straining forward to what lies ahead.' [Philippians 3:13]   —Origen

A T this moment Jesus' look became so inwardly and upwardly directed that I knew he saw things none of us could grasp. He comprehended what the kingdom of God really was, but he could only tell us what it was like. To make his point, he would ask us to hold in our minds opposite images as when he compared something of such greatness as the reign of God to a mustard seed. It was a mere speck in the cosmos, but when it grew under the loving eye of its Creator, it became a large bush and "the birds of the air made nests in its branches" [Luke 13:19].

As if he were back in the coziness of our kitchen in Nazareth, where he loved to help me knead dough and bake bread, he made us think of God's reign as a measure of yeast! One portion of it in three measures of flour would cause the whole mass of dough to rise [see Luke 13:21].

What were we to make of these comparisons? What did they mean? For what were we praying when we asked in silence or spoke aloud, "Thy kingdom come?"

This was not the first time I had heard such comparisons—though indeed these are among the easiest to remember. When we took our many country walks when he was young, he would dream of the time he could share with others his visions and convictions of the ages to come. He foresaw an age freed from fear, violence, hatred, and ill will. He wanted his followers to taste and see the goodness of God's reign already on earth.

As he spoke of these things, he would cradle in his palm the little gifts nature yields when one walks the fields: a grain of wheat, a pebble made smooth and shiny by the rain, a fallen leaf.

"Look, Mother," he would say, "how small and insignificant these things are. Yet I tell you they radiate God's glory. If only people could imitate the generosity of my Father, there would be no wars between them. Such seeds cover the earth. Such pebbles line the shores. Such leaves fall on good and bad ground alike. Yet people don't see them! In their quest for earthly power and possession everything my Father made is trampled upon. O, Mother! If only they would keep his promise in their hearts, peace could be proclaimed even in this war-torn land of ours!"

As much as I loved to share such observations with him, I also cherished these silent exchanges beyond words that drew us closer together. He stood near a small plot of ground apparently spellbound by what he saw. I had walked over to bring him something to drink because he had been in the sun for a long time, just sitting and praying. As I approached, a twig snapped. He looked over his shoulder and saw me. He smiled and motioned me to join him, placing his fingers on his lips to signal me that it was not the time to speak.

I bent over to see the object to which he was pointing and a gasp of delight escaped my lips. Somehow a tiny blade of grass had pushed its way through a crevice in a huge boulder. There it stood like a brave soldier crossing a barren desert— undaunted by all the forces lined up against it, stretching toward the sun as a symbol of new life, defying the odds pressing for death.

Did he see in that tiny greening a symbol of his own life, of the mission soon to be thrust upon him, of his desire to reveal that amidst situations, impossible by human calculations, the reign would have its time? Did he know, even then, that the hope of the ages he embodied would only mean something when everything around us appeared to be hopeless?

Much as I knew his mind, even I could only speculate about what he pondered in his heart. My part was to pray with urgency and confident expectancy that the kingdom of God was at hand, that the people would repent, that we would, singularly and in solidarity, give birth to the new beginning my Son was soon to proclaim.

His cousin, John, did not hesitate for a moment to say what had to be done. He came out of the desert on fire with the love of God. The desert does such things to prophets. It gets inside their minds and changes them forever. It recrafts their language. Their words, though few, are always true.

John came forth from his nights and days of solitary prayer and fasting hearing the one word necessary: "Repent, for the kingdom of heaven has come near" [Matthew 3:2].

People were stunned. They stopped in their tracks. Their entire life flashed before them. Many experienced a lasting conversion of heart. They were ready to behold in Jesus, the Messiah generations had foretold.

Jesus knew their hearts. He even told Joseph and me, when we read the scriptures together and commented on them, that he feared people wanted a worldly savior—a man of power who would crush the enemy and set them free until the next conqueror came along. He prayed that they would understand the metaphor of the mustard seed: that his kingdom was not of this world; that it had to be built from scratch by the grace of God in the depths of their hearts; that it was up to them to change the world from a place of alienation from the Most High to a kingdom where love knew no bounds.

What parables he told in the hope that his message would be heard! Yet how deaf were the ears on which these luminous words of his would fall! I rejoice for the many who received the message as only repentant sinners can. They understood that God's reign was already at hand [see Luke 17:21]. They were like the sensible bridesmaids who kept their oil lamps burning so that when the groom came they would be ready to greet him [see Matthew 25:1-13]. They were like the guests who came to the banquet prepared by the king; others, though invited, made foolish excuses not to come. Such was not the case with the faithful ones: they were waiting on the highways and byways for an invitation. Even though it came at the last minute, they dressed properly and went to the party! [see Matthew 22:1-14].

What a genius Jesus was to think of such wonderful stories. People never forgot them. They were literally astonished at his teaching [see Matthew 22:33]. That's what happened the day he taught us to pray.

A man and his wife, two among the many listeners visibly touched by his teaching, approached me later that day to share an astonishing interpretation of what they had heard, especially when the three words, "Thy kingdom come," were uttered.

On one level, they knew they were beseeching the most high God to come among them. On another level, this petition made them remember their own dignity in the eyes of the Father. He said to her, she said to him, in whispers ringing with newfound hope, "Come into the fullness of your call from God. Shed every shadow of self-pity. Accept that you are worthy to sit at God's table."

It was a delight to behold the genuine excitement in their eyes. It was as if all of us had stepped from one dimension of life into another—as if we were already in some way in heaven, hallowing God's name but also hallowing in one another the awareness of the Divine Presence, freed from the constrictions of time-bound expectations.

I beheld in the members of our little flock not only inner lights of insight but also touches of genuine urgency. Was the hour of their salvation really at hand?

Now that my dearest child has died and risen, the community of faith is one in its trust that he has saved them from their sins and that he will come again. The "when" of this promise is not ours to know. With a sigh, at times even a groan, the best of believers had to let go of their penchant for predictability and return to prayer. The peace of Jesus settled upon them and they were content to wait upon God's will. They took to heart the commission they received in this "between" time, between his resurrection and the second coming, to live in the here and now of God's reign.

It comes whenever a Good Samaritan bandages a victim's wounds; whenever a nursing mother bends over a sick child; whenever strangers or friends clothe the naked and feed the hungry; whenever pastors shepherd their flock or truth prevails over falsehood or violence melts in the face of love. Then the reign of God is at hand and all the suffering my Son endured to advance its coming is like purifying fire. In its heat, idolatrous kingdoms [see Isaiah 10:10] crumble to dust and fertile soil reappears—soil in which mustard seeds can be planted.

I sit now in the shade of this lovely tree. It is cool here. A light breeze fans my face. Birds nestle in its branches and sing songs at once melodious and melancholy. They make me feel like a child again, forever young, at least in heart. No worldly riches restrain me, no semblance of recognition. My eyes strain toward him whom I love with my whole heart and soul. Today I hear his voice assuring me that salvation has come to this house [see Luke 19:9].

EXPECTATION

In Nazareth I felt
the divine bent
of each event
in my unfolding days.
I listened in expectation
to the synagogue's sources
of holy inspiration.
I did all I could
to make with Jesus
my work at home one
with Father's will
watching in faith
the unveiling
of my call of life.

I was in love
with those to whom
God would impart
a new start of life.
Now I begin
every morning
in sweet surrender.
I treasure in my heart
my Son's decision
in spite of derision
never to lose sight
of Father's promised reign
in the midst of suffering
and pain.

Dwelling in this pagan city
my heart swells with pity
for all who do not know him yet
still dwell in his debt.

I do not mind being
once again a woman
in waiting, every memory
pierced by an agony
of longing for him.

Strange as it may seem, my heart
is more and more enwrapped
in wondrous elation.
He shall be Lord of every tribe and nation,
over people abiding
in any station. All are
called to salvation,
the fulfillment begun
by my beloved Son.
He never wearies
of intimacy
with suffering humanity.

My children, hear my plea,
walk with me expectantly,
do not faint or flee,
look forward
to the Revelation of his glory
elevating your daily story
of pain and worry,
marvel at the epiphany
of his compassion with humanity.

CHAPTER FIVE

Renunciation

"Thy Will Be Done on Earth as it is in Heaven"

So then it is clear that Christ is calling his disciples to work faithfully with him by means of their prayers. That all earthly events may come to be transformed by the authority that Christ has received both in heaven and on earth, this ought to be our prayer.

—Origen

JESUS said these words not only with his lips but with his entire body. He stretched his arms to heaven, as I would one day see them stretched on the cross. He stood before us in silent surrender. The words welled up from his inmost being. He whispered them a second time in a barely audible voice.

With a mother's watchful eye, I saw beads of sweat appear on his brow, though it was a cool day. Even I could not have foreseen what he intuited as he bowed before us in a gesture of utter self-renunciation and prayer. His words foretold his agonized utterance in the Garden of Gethsemane, "Father, if you are willing, remove this cup from me; yet, not my will but yours be done" [Luke 13:42].

Were I able to place the depth of my Son's surrender on a scale, its weight would surpass the highest conceivable measure. In all humility, I know he would say the same of me!

There is perhaps no more important word in our speaking together, indeed in our entire family's exchanges, than "obedience." It is the word that rivets us to God.

Union of our wills with God's gave us the energy we needed to flee to Egypt when Jesus' life was in danger. After we found him in the temple several years later, he stayed with us and was himself obedient to us [see Luke 2:51]. Indeed, obedience was behind the conviction we felt that our obscure life in Nazareth would bear much fruit. It was sheer obedience that drew me to ponder these things in all their significance deep in my heart.

Waiting upon the Lord, despite what some may think, is not a passive act, will-less, and without courage. It is among the most difficult things a free human being can do.

I remember catching Jesus many times at the window of our house, "watching the world go by," as he would say. One day I saw him shake his head with sadness. "My Son," I said with empathy, "Why are you troubled?" He replied, with words I later realized were prophetic, that the people were like sheep without a shepherd [see Matthew 9:36]. They were rushing to and fro, buying and selling, hoarding as many goods as they could, neglecting the poor, thinking mainly of themselves, hardly ever pausing to pray and listen to God's word. Yet "Let anyone with ears to hear listen" [Luke 8:8].

Both of us wanted to shout the truth from the rooftops, but we chose instead to watch and pray. In God's time, not ours, with God's words, not human utterances, he would preach the unexpected, teach the truth, challenge a recalcitrant flock to renounce the wide way of perdition and come to God through the "narrow door" [Luke 22:24] of obedience.

For a moment motherly care overtook me. After all, I had once held a tall, strong teenager in my arms. Seeds of wisdom, age, and grace took root in his heart [see Luke 2:52]. He learned obedience through suffering [see Hebrews 5:8]. It was a hard lesson we who followed him would have to learn time and again in silent lamentation.

People have asked me often enough a question I find amusing: "Please, Mary, tell us in a word, what was Jesus' message?" I answer, "Let me tell you in two words. It was: 'Yes, Father.'" I always felt that in Jesus' "Yes" there was contained an antidote to every "No" that had ever been said to God from the beginning of time. I knew that his stalwart "Yes" was like a bulwark against the evil forces of corruption that led to the Fall of humankind.

Often I would awaken in the depths of the night and find him almost visibly engaged in a cosmic struggle with every disobedient presence in the universe. The more these forces pulled against God's will, the harder Jesus prayed. He called upon the Father to show mercy for our sins. He offered himself as a willing sacrifice. He desired with his whole being, even if it meant his death, to reconcile fallen humanity to the Father's will.

I would kneel beside him as his silent prayer companion. In due course, as if a calming hand had quieted a tempest, peace would flood our domain. Believe it or not, amidst tears of lamentation, we would start to laugh.

Once he turned and took my hands, gently lifted me from the floor, and swung me around the room in a joyful, breathless, traditional dance. Music could be heard, surely in our hearts, because at that time of night who could be playing their fiddle?

We woke Joseph with our frolicking and he joined the dance. It was such a marvelous moment! Even to remember it sets these old feet of mine tapping.

This is the dance of life over which death has no power. When he said we were to pray, "Thy will be done," I knew exactly what he meant. In this simple phrase would be voiced our faith that the victory over evil belongs to God.

What God willed—our good, our salvation, the forgiveness of sins—would be done. For this purpose my child had come into the world. Life was to be lived everyday in accordance with God's loving will. Then heaven would descend to earth. Then earth would ascend heavenward.

Jesus wanted his disciples to experience no separation between his and their "Yes" to the Father. I think this is what he meant when he said: "If any want to become my followers, let them deny themselves and take up their cross and follow me" [Mark 8:34].

What could be farther from self-glorification than this pledge of self-renunciation? The apostles were twelve good and brave souls, but few knew what it was like, before Jesus came into their lives, to fight the hardest battle of all: the struggle against their own willfulness and pride.

It was human to think they knew better. Even Peter, dear as he was, tried to prevent Jesus from going up to Jerusalem [see Matthew 16:22]. Poor man! He knew Jesus was the Messiah [see Matthew 16:16] and still he judged things by human standards, not by God's [see Matthew 16:23].

Liberation from sin is the greatest gift God can give his people. His greatest joy is to see us give everything we are and do to him, holding nothing back as on that day when I gave him the gift of my own permanent "Yes."

That "May it be" [see Luke 1:38] was utterly free. That's the kind of obedience Jesus wanted from his followers: nothing coerced, nothing given begrudgingly. Perhaps that is why he pointed so often to the birds of the air and the flowers of the field. They delighted the Father's eye.

Though the soil around our house was dry and at first glance not too fertile, we always planted flowers and vegetables. Jesus would do the watering, pruning, and replanting. Flower arrangements adorned our table all year long. Fresh vegetables were a staple of our diet.

I often thought that if Jesus could have chosen another profession than carpentry it would have been shepherding or farming. He loved animals and they loved him. He could hardly take a walk down the street without a variety of creatures following him, dogs and cats and, to the dismay of a few neighbors, their lambs! Of course, he would return these wobbly babes to the sheepfold, wrapping them tenderly around his neck in a gesture of gentleness forever etched in my memory.

"If only people would take a lesson from these wondrous creatures," he would say. "My Father in heaven wants all on earth to act in concert with his will for their good. O my people, unstrap the shackles from your wrists. Let me release you from your bondage to sin. Let me set you free. Can't you see: If God clothes in such splendor the grass of the field, which grows today and is thrown on the fire tomorrow, how much more will he provide for you, O weak in faith!" [see Luke 12:28].

Now, in full recollection of the depths to which obedience took my Son, I am comforted by beholding the simple treasures of the earth. Each morning the sun rises, each evening it sets. Stars appear; a stream of light from the moon bathes the gravel in a luminescent glow; dew drops nestle on each blade of grass that struggles for moisture in this dry land. The cosmos is in perfect harmony with its Creator. Nothing on earth is only what it appears to be; it is always much more—a veritable epiphany that discloses to the obedient the heart of God.

Earth and heaven bow before him in praise and adoration. In my mind's eye I see the thousands of souls who have been touched by my Son's message. With them I pray, "Yes, Father. Thy will, not mine be done."

The cross of renunciation is what brings us to the mount of transfiguration. There we experience what it means to be truly free. Though one's body may be given up for burning, one's spirit belongs to God. No enemy can penetrate this final citadel where we are with God and God is with us.

RENUNCIATION

Lady of Epiphany
haunting melody echoing
Father's supplication,
to love creation
while living Christ's renunciation.
Your image invites us
day after day
to the wide open way
that nothing can fill
but his holy will.
Jesus' birth
now assures our worth
us daughters and sons
who say and pray:
God's will be done,
on earth as in heaven.
Don't let us fall
into the sea
of wild desire,
its scorching fire
cutting the wire with divinity,
causing strife
with his love will
in our life.
Silently sensing
where our will is tending,
we beg you, Mother,
teach us to bear
Father's condemnation of a life
of self-centered strife.
In renunciation
let us share the
wear and tear
of your immolation.

CHAPTER SIX

Donation

"Give Us this Day
Our Daily Bread"

The Lord's Prayer speaks of 'daily' bread. In saying that, let us
remember that the life in which we ought to be interested is
'daily' life. We can, each of us, only call the present time our own.
Why should we worry ourselves by thinking about the future?

—Gregory of Nyssa

THIS petition touched such a deep chord in the people
crowding around Jesus that a tremor passed through them
when he said it. His listeners, myself included, were schooled in
the scriptures. Genesis, Exodus, Leviticus, Numbers, Deuteronomy—these books lived in our blood. The Torah guided our
lives. The Covenant kept the flame of hope burning in us however hopeless life seemed. The Commandments brought order
to the chaos caused by amoral, avaricious, lustful behavior,
betraying God and bringing misery to women and men.

One of the fondest recollections I have from my own childhood was when my mother, Anna, took me on her lap, and we
listened to the majestic voice of my father, Joachim, as he read
the Bible and gave us time to reflect on each text and story.

I have many favorites: Noah finally coming to dry land after forty days and nights of rain [see Genesis 8:6-13]; Moses descending from the mountaintop with the sacred tablets in his hand [see Exodus 32:15]; Sarah being with child in her old age [see Genesis 17:15-21].

One story moves me in a special way. I believe the reason is that there were times in my youth—due either to famine or fasting—when I knew both physical and spiritual hunger. I longed for a morsel of bread to nourish my body as the bread of God's word nourished my soul.

Israel's is a story of near despair and of prayer rising to heaven. In it one hears hungry groans and grumbles oblivious, at least momentarily, to the promises of God. The Israelites have been roaming in the Sinai desert for months. Their food supplies are dwindling. Shrunken stomachs become more important than shared and sacred concerns. Moses and Aaron are demoted by the people from rescuers to reckless adventurers. Everyone whines and complains: "If only we had died by the hand of the Lord in the land of Egypt, when we sat by the fleshpots and ate our fill of bread; for you have brought us out into this wilderness to kill this whole assembly with hunger" [Exodus 16:3].

My father Joachim articulated these words in such a way that we felt we were in that desert, too. He made us mindful by the sheer resonance of his voice of what it means to lose hope, to doubt the fidelity of God, to question the depth of divine love.

What would the Lord's response be to this collective cry? Not vengeance, not retribution, but the bounty, the utter generosity, of divine donation: "I am going to rain bread from heaven for you, and each day the people shall go out and gather enough for that day. In that way I will test them, whether they will follow my instruction or not" [Exodus 16:4]. Manna would diminish their hunger in the morning. "In the evening quails came up and covered the camp; and in the morning

there was a layer of dew around the camp" [Exodus 16:13].
Meat would manage their need at night. God gave the people
their daily fare despite the doubt he read in their hearts. They
prayed. God gave. His generosity could not be undone then
nor need we doubt it now.

With bread we also celebrated the greatest feast in our tradition: the Passover. Every Jewish child remembers this awesome ceremony. I can still taste the unleavened bread we ate.
With each bite we recalled our liberation by the Lord from
bondage and humiliation. Jesus told me every year how much
he treasured this time at our own family table. How could I
have known then that he himself would be the sacrificial lamb,
that his body and blood would be the bread and wine at the
center of our paschal feast?

"My Child," I whispered to myself as he prayed, "You are
the manna of mercy sent from heaven. You are the bread of life
whose body broken for us becomes the surest sign of God's
devotion to us."

When Jesus told us to pray for daily bread, I was struck, as
I had often been, by the shape of his hands. He had beautiful-
ly formed, elongated fingers, at once strong and tender. He
could wield a heavy hammer or stroke a butterfly's wing.

When he helped me in the kitchen, he admitted that his
favorite task was bread making. He loved to shape the dough
and watch it bake with or without yeast, depending on its purpose in our diet.

After John baptized him in the Jordan, when he felt
renewed in body and spirit, he went into the desert for forty
days. I foresaw that he would undergo a time of testing and
that he would be transformed by prayer. Motherly solicitude
made me want to give him some food, but one look told me he
had already made up his mind to take nothing with him.

As he later related, this was a time of agony and ecstasy. He
was hungry and, from a human point of view, vulnerable. The

Devil took his physical hunger as a sign that perhaps he was too weak to resist defeat. He taunted Jesus, "If you are the Son of God command this stone to become a loaf of bread" [Luke 4:3]. Did he really think Jesus would fall for such a ruse? Did he not realize that my Son had been fed from his earliest days by the holy bread of God's word?

The answer Jesus gave now lives in the memory of our faith community. People often repeat it when they are tempted by the lesser gods of power, pleasure, and possession: "Scripture has it: 'One does not live by bread alone, but by every word that comes from the mouth of God' " [Matthew 4:4].

There were two other temptations Jesus had to withstand but, with this first reply, the Devil was already defeated. We were, of course, surrounded by every conceivable form of poverty in Nazareth: poverty of body in diseases like leprosy and so many crippling conditions—deafness, blindness, paralysis—and poverty of spirit crushing people with the weight of aggression, oppression, despair, and every kind of indignity.

As far back as I can remember, Jesus responded to the misery of people with complete mercy. If they thirsted, he ran to the well to give them a drink. If they were in mourning, he spent time comforting them. Never did a beggar who came to our door asking for bread go away hungry.

No wonder one of the greatest miracles Jesus ever performed had to do with feeding the multitudes. I knew how tired he was. One look at his face told me he longed for the healing air of desert solitude, for the sweet balm of silence, but it was not to be. As soon as the crowds got wind of where he was, they followed him. How could he turn away so vast a throng? Not when the sight of them moved his heart to pity. Not when their sicknesses needed to be cured.

Thinking of his best interest, the apostles wanted him, as evening was drawing near, to dismiss the crowds. After all, it was they who had followed him to this deserted place. They got there on their two feet and, hungry or not, they could go home the same way.

This mindset, reasonable as it seemed, was not my Son's way. He told his astonished band to find them something to eat.

What could he mean? No one could feed a crowd of five thousand with "five loaves and two fish" [see Matthew 14:17]. It wasn't as if people had packed picnic baskets! What did he expect them to do—turn stones into bread!

I must say one of the remarkable virtues Jesus had was patience. He overlooked their puzzlement, their voiced and unvoiced complaints. He asked them simply and politely to bring to him what they had. The crowds sensed a special aura surrounding him. Hungry and unruly as they were at first, one by one they sat on the grass.

Then he took those loaves and fishes in his hands and, looking up to heaven, he blessed them, broke them, and gave them to the disciples to distribute to the people. The awe in the atmosphere was palpable. Many cried while they ate, remembering the story of the manna in the desert that fed their hungry ancestors. They ate until they were full and still there were twelve baskets of leftovers.

Word of this miraculous food spread far and wide. Many followed Jesus because they were fed. They did not yet grasp the fuller sense of what he would ask. That test came later. Some stayed, but many more turned away.

It was one thing to eat table food, quite another to hear someone call himself "the bread of life" [John 6:35]. What kind of teaching was that? What did he mean by saying that to come to him meant never to be hungry? That to believe in him meant never to thirst? Were they fools? Was he playing tricks with their minds with this talk of eternal life and of being raised up on the last day? Wasn't this the son of Joseph, the carpenter and of that good woman, Mary? Who was he to claim, "I have come down from heaven" [John 6:42]?

The same people who once gave thanks for the bread he gave them, now grumbled. There were times when he could walk away and leave people pondering their own questions, but this was not one of them. He persisted in his proclamation that he was the living bread and that anyone who ate the flesh of the Son of Man and drank his blood would have life eternal. Imagine how shocked almost everyone in the synagogue was when he said, "for my flesh is true food, and my blood is true drink" [John 6:55].

My child needed friends. We all do. I know it hurt him when even his closest followers found such talk hard to endure. He knew this teaching would shake their faith, and it did. This in a way was his parting of the Red Sea moment since from this time on, many of the disciples broke away and would not remain in his company any longer [see John 6:66].

It makes me sad to remember how few of us were left at the foot of the Cross. I believe what held us together was the miracle of the Last Supper when he blessed and broke the bread that was his body, when he consecrated the wine that was his blood. As I held his broken body in my arms, it consoled me to think that he would be with us always in the breaking of the bread. This sacred meal would be our daily fare. The fruit of the vine and the work of human hands, wine and bread, offered in remembrance of him, would become his body and blood. Just as he had foretold, it would bring us to everlasting life.

Let me cease now with this reminiscing. It feels like forever since I rose from bed this morning. I look forward to enjoying a piece of my home baked bread. I slice it, hold it reverently in my hands in thanksgiving, and bite into its goodness. For some reason, I start to weep. I sense how near to me my child is. His spirit gives me life [see John 6:63], but I am a mother, and I miss our meals together.

DONATION

Mary, make me venerate
Father's donations in my life,
Be they small or great,
Even if I have long to wait.

Mary, make me imitate
your gratefulness for gifts poured out
on teeming shores
of generosity beyond imagining.

Mary, make me adore
The mystery of holy energy,
of God-given potency
playing in cosmos and humanity.

Mary, meek and mild,
bearing for a while
the pains of exile
in a foreign land,
under the guiding love of Father's hand.
Soon the Trinity
will crown thee for eternity
as Mother of the mystery.

Now on earth
I bend my knee
before the daily gift
of Eucharist:
Christ's body and blood,
soul and divinity
Granted to all who believe
every time they receive.

CHAPTER SEVEN

Reconciliation

"And Forgive Us Our Trespasses"

The mercy of God is beyond description. While he is offering us a model prayer he is teaching us a way of life whereby we can be pleasing in his sight. —John Cassian

"FORGIVE us" was the petition Jesus wanted to hear on the lips of his listeners. Vendors, vagrants, officers of the guard, offenders against the law were among the many people who repeated his words silently or aloud. All longed for release from the bondage of past mistakes and present entanglements.

A return to that purity the Father intended for his children before the Fall is not possible for sinful human beings, but liberation through love is a goal reachable through God's grace. Forgiveness depended on their faith in Jesus. Did they believe that God is love [see John 1:4] and that he seeks reconciliation with repentant people?

Jesus' entire life could be described as a ministry of forgiveness. In the face of the old law, he proclaimed a new set of commandments founded on the bedrock of forgiveness.

Our people had been taught for generations to take an eye for an eye and a tooth for a tooth. But Jesus said: ". . .Love

your enemies, and pray for those who persecute you . . ."
[Matthew 5:44].

I remember an episode that happened in our old neighborhood. Two brothers began feuding over possessions. Their anger worsened so much that we feared for their life. Jesus stepped in. He brought them over to our house, sat them at the table, gave them something to drink, and began gently but firmly to penetrate the wall of accusations behind which each of them stubbornly stood. Jesus helped them to see each other's view of the situation while finding the common ground upon which they could agree. By the time they left, they had begun to break down the walls between them and to rebuild relationships that would help them to overcome their vehement opposition.

The lessons learned by this and similar experiences led to some of the most unforgettable moments in Jesus' teaching, all involving forgiveness. The brothers knew quite well what he meant when he said, "... leave your gift there before the altar and go; first be reconciled to your brother or sister, and then come and offer your gift" [Matthew 5:23-24].

Jesus could be mild about many things, but on matters such as this he did not bend. He left no doubt in the minds of his disciples as to what such demands meant. "Come to terms quickly with your accuser..." [Matthew 5:25]. And, taking matters a step farther, he said, "...if anyone strikes you on the right cheek, turn the other also..." [Matthew 5:39].

Jesus and I had the chance to see forgiveness in action in the life of Joseph. I knew from experience the pain every snide remark about our relationship caused him, yet I never heard a harsh word of judgment pass his lips. He had the patience of a saint and the knack of placing himself in other's shoes. "Mary, can you blame them for misjudging us? They have no way of understanding what we know to be true. Were the veil lifted from their eyes, it would be impossible for them to behave so badly. Let's just forgive them and forget about it. God will illumine their minds in his own good time."

It would have come as no surprise to Joseph that from the cross itself, when Jesus could have chosen to condemn his accusers, he not only forgave one of the criminals who hung beside him [see Luke 23:37-43]; he also uttered the words that sealed his mission of salvation: "Father, forgive them; for they do not know what they are doing" [Luke 23:34].

The very powerlessness of Jesus released in people like the good thief that hung beside him the power to ask for forgiveness. Unless the hearts of sinners are broken by repentance, they cannot be healed. Into the cup of compunction, chipped as it may be, Jesus can pour the wine of forgiveness. Until people know how thirsty they are, they cannot drink fully from it.

Repentant sinners were attracted to my Son like dry grasses to the rain, people like the paralytic who rose and walked after Jesus said to him, "Take heart, son; your sins are forgiven" [Matthew 9:2].

There were two encounters, both with women, that are still recounted as vividly as on the day they occurred. People see in them excellent examples of Jesus' commitment to practice every word he preached. Jesus was sensitive to women, who were often treated as objects of desire or branded as public sinners. The way he treated them was life changing.

One of these women had been accused of committing adultery. It had been determined by the scribes and pharisees that stoning her was the only fit punishment. They would show her then and there who was righteous and who was despicable. One look at the hatred in their faces and Jesus concluded this was no time to argue with them. Instead he "bent down and wrote with his finger on the ground" [John 8:6]. As their murmuring grew louder, he countered not with an accusation but with a simple statement: "Let anyone among you who is without sin be the first to throw a stone at her" [John 8:7]. Silence fell like a blanket as he resumed writing in the sand. No sooner had the elders and the others deciphered his markings then one by one they walked away.

Jesus and the woman were alone. He looked into her eyes and saw both fear and foreboding. Where were the men who wanted to condemn her? They were no where to be seen. In that quiet, healing space between her and Jesus, he spoke the words she needed most to hear. "Neither do I condemn. Go your way, and from now on do not sin again" [John 8:11].

I wish I had seen the look on her face when she felt forgiven. Not only did Jesus refuse to condemn her. He went a step further and forgave her. He freed her to begin her life anew from this point on. It was as if he said to her: "As you go forth from this place of disgrace and diminishment of your dignity, let go of all that stands between you and God. Don't be a slave to your own desires but a free woman committed to fulfilling God's hopes for you. Untie the tangled knots that bound you to wrong relationships. Learn to respect yourself. Go and be reconciled with the God who forgives you not seven times but seventy seven times!" [see Matthew 18:22].

Jesus did a good thing for this woman, but another sinner like her did something out of pure goodness for him. It happened on a social occasion. One of the pharisees had invited him to dinner. As was the custom, he reclined at table, probably in expectation of the questions his host would soon ask him. It seemed strange to him that, as was also the custom, he had been offered no water in which to wash his hands and feet. Suddenly, against all customs, a woman of obviously ill repute knelt before him, her face wet with weeping. In a gesture of sincere repentance for her sins and respect for Jesus, she cleansed the dust from his feet with her tears, dried them with her hair, and anointed them with precious oil from the alabaster flask she carried with her.

A gasp went up from the guests. How could he let this sort of woman touch him? He paid them no mind until they stopped whispering. Then he told them a brief but powerful story about the generosity of a creditor who forgave a person unable to pay him the debt he owed. He impressed upon them how grateful that debtor felt and then made his point.

When he had arrived at Simon's house, he was not so much as given water to bathe his feet, but she washed them with her tears and dried them with her hair. He did not receive a welcoming kiss, but she had not ceased kissing his feet. No one even thought to anoint his head with oil, but she chose spontaneously to soothe his tired feet by rubbing them with this perfumed balm. Though no words were exchanged between them, Jesus knew what she was asking for. It was a gift only he could give.

In the company of Simon and all the other invited guests, he said both to her and to them: "Therefore, I tell you, her sins, which were many, have been forgiven; hence she has shown great love. But the one to whom little is forgiven, loves little" [Luke 7:47]. In gratitude for her show of great love, he would bestow upon her the gift of great forgiveness.

In the lives of both of these women, the weight of sin had been lifted, restoring their vision of God, self, and others. That's the way Jesus was. That's the kind of thing he did best, leading people from the dead end streets of sin's debt to the open spaces of new starts.

Once, when he asked for my advice as to where his life might be taking him, I said: "My Son, you will draw to yourself not only the ill of body but the sick of soul. You will look beyond the ugliness of sin to the beauty of redemption and all who seek this gift sincerely will be your disciples, forgiving others as you forgave them." He smiled at my prediction, knowing in his heart that it was already true.

RECONCILIATION

Mother, listen to your child
when my moods seem strange and wild.
Ask Jesus for relief,
him to whom I pray for peace.
Unwind the bondage
of my restless mind,
forgive my sin, that I may win
with the baptized of Ephesus
the reconciliation Jesus gained
in the evening of his pained
yet victorious life
spent in our midst.

Teach me the Gospel story:
let it quell my anger
still my worry.
Show me a way
no longer to stray
from forgiveness and love.

Forgiveness was for you
the jewel of the beatitudes
with which
God enriched your spotless heart.
Teach me how to bear
without bitterness, with your good cheer
the snide remarks
unbelievers aim at me.
Reconciliation has the power
to free both friend and enemy.
How could people know
that every hammer blow
on your son's bleeding body
still echoes in your soul?

Pained by their indignation,
you prayed for reconciliation,
repeating the words of your child:
"Father, forgive them too,
for they know not what they do."
Let your Son's grace flow through
me as it flowed through you.

Place my heart in his wounded side.
Where the wine of forgiveness streams out
like the ebb and flow of a holy tide
in every crevice and space
of a race hollowed out by a thirst
for God's appreciation,
his reconciliation.

Mary, ask Jesus to create in me
a slate wiped clean
of the dark and dreary dream
of revenge, of condemnation.

Chapter Eight

Transformation

"As We Forgive Those Who Trespass Against Us"

If we are faithful in this prayer, each of us will ask forgiveness for our own failings after we have forgiven the sins of those who have sinned against us. I mean those who have sinned against us, not only those who have sinned against our Master. —John Cassian

M Y Son said these words solemnly and slowly as if he foresaw that the demand inherent in them he, too, would have to fulfill under circumstances defying any semblance of civility.

I can still see the light, the sheer joy, on his face as he taught us to pray that day. Had I known then what it would mean for him to choose for our sake to follow the way of love, I do not know if I could have endured it.

On Calvary the beauty of his demeanor would discolor due to the dark lashes of human sin, yet every scar on his body would become a new star in the heaven of forgiveness.

How proud I am of him! Not even pain as perverse as that of the cross could prevent him from witnessing to a truth more profound than his tormentors could fathom. The louder they shouted, the more they spat upon him and called him names, the quieter he became. His answer to noise was silence, to anger, love, to cruelty, compassion. His teaching from the cross resembled the crescendo of a grand symphony where the music draws us from death's grip to life's release. Words of mercy formed on his quivering lips. We heard him say in an almost inaudible whisper, "Father, forgive them; for they do not know what they are doing" [Luke 23:34].

Jesus taught us to pray for the wisdom and courage to forgive people whose behavior threatens to trap us in prisons of anger. He understood how hardened hearts can become when people are treated badly.

In those days we Jews were like pawns on the chessboard of a conquering power. Injustice and oppression were as common as dust blowing from the desert. A sense of despair hung in the air. To rob, cheat, assassinate, curse, find a scapegoat, slaughter the innocent were solutions that made sense to many. But to forgive the enemy as God forgave us—Never! Absurd! It was beyond what one could ask of mere mortals, but it was what Jesus expected us to do and what he proved could be done by his own example.

I admit as a mother that I pray every day for the grace to forgive the people who did what they did to him. Forgiveness transforms us, he taught. Holding on to the hurt makes us ill. Sometimes there are no words on my lips, only tears so plentiful they form rivulets on my face.

I remember a merchant in our village for whom Jesus felt great compassion. Even as a boy, he could make friends with anyone, but this man turned and went the other way whenever he saw him. One day Jesus was standing with me as the merchant rounded a corner, spotted us from afar, and ducked into an alley.

"My Son, he doesn't know you that well. Of what is he afraid?"

The answer alerted me to why some people, years later, for reasons that defied any semblance of logic, would scream when Pontius Pilate offered to release him, "Let him be crucified!" [Matthew 27:22].

He may not have known the merchant as he knew our relatives and friends, but he saw what was in his heart: "He cannot forgive his wife, nor the man for whom she left him. Hatred is the only force holding his life together. When he sees love alive as in you and me, he cannot bear the sight of it. So he runs away—from God, from the other members of his family, and, worst of all, from himself. Let's pray that he finds a way to forgive them and to leave their judgment to God. Otherwise he may never know a moment's peace."

I felt a blessing go out from him to this poor soul. No wonder we were tired at the end of the day. There were so many people for whom we prayed.

Whenever I'm asked to summarize the final years of Jesus' life on earth, I feel drawn to repeat this part of the prayer: "He forgave those who trespassed against him." All of their faces are before me: Judas, Pilate, the pharisees and sadducees who plotted against him, Peter, the crowds who lined the way to the cross—every murmurer, doubter, tormentor, jailer, the soldiers who pounded the nails into his hands and feet, the thief hanging beside him, sinners past, present, and to come, everyone who ever asked or would ask for the dispensation to be found in the healing power of forgiveness.

Does it make any sense to ask God to forgive one's sins and then for us to turn around and refuse to forgive their offenses?

So new was this commandment that Jesus had to reiterate it—in this prayer, with admonitions and through parables. He told the disciples one day, "If another sins, you must rebuke the offender, and if there is repentance, you must forgive" [Luke 17:3]. This was like saying, "Hate the sin, don't condone betrayal or any form of outright badness, but love the sinner. Expect him to feel repentance, if not now, then later. Pray that his conscience will lead him to tell the truth. Even before he repents, be ready to forgive him." Then Jesus took this revolutionary teaching one step further. "And if the same person sins against you seven times a day, and turns back to you seven times and says, 'I repent,' you must forgive" [Luke 17:4].

No wonder the apostles' only reply to this imperative was, "Increase our faith!" [Luke 17:5]. It takes great faith to remove from human hearts the wall of unforgiveness that often remains impenetrable to love.

Faith in Jesus, in his power of forgiveness, alone makes it possible to forgive the people who trespass against us. Reconciliation, not revenge, was his way of resolving differences.

The wonderful parable of the prodigal son is a lesson in love. The character who most needed to learn it was the elder son. His wayward, younger brother had sunk to despicable lows in his life experiences. Either he had to repent and forgive himself and return to his father's house seeking forgiveness or die forgotten and despised in a foreign land. When he chose the former course and fell into the compassionate arms of his father, his trespasses were forgiven and forgotten. It was as if they had never occurred.

No wonder a bolt of resentment gripped the elder brother's heart. Luckily for him, his father intervened before this poison spread through his system like an ulcer of unforgiveness. He did not deny the trespasses of his younger son. He had done everything of which he had accused himself and probably more. So shameful were his secret sins and guilt that only God knew of them. But that was not the point. Another chapter in their lives still had to be written.

In the face of the lies and devastation sin leaves in its wake, the father said to him, "Son, you are always with me; and all that is mine is yours. But we had to celebrate and rejoice, because this brother of yours was dead and has come to life; he was lost and has been found" [Luke 15:31-32].

A story was worth more than a thousand words when it came to teaching lessons people found hard to swallow. Jesus knew our nature so well! Even as a boy in Nazareth, he was the one to whom the locals would come to settle a spat. The smallest thing could set off the firecracker of unforgiveness—a promise made to meet someone at a certain time and place, only not to show up; a lie told and retold to procure more than a deal was worth; a friend trusted, who sets one up as the brunt of a cruel joke.

Complaints about nearly everything were laid at Jesus' feet from morning to night: "People who don't keep their word are useless, I want nothing to do with them! What did I do to deserve such treatment? I'll show them the next time who gets the last laugh!"

One story he loved to tell exploded the myth of "this for that" and forced people to acknowledge the outrageous depth of divine generosity [see Matthew 20:1-16]. It had to do with workers in the vineyard. One morning the master of the vineyard hired workers for the day and agreed to pay them a set amount. Three hours or so later he saw that he needed more helpers. He agreed to pay them the same, and so it was for the sixth and the ninth and finally the eleventh hour. The workers who started later had much less to do, but they did what they were told.

When it came time to collect their wages, all lined up, from those hired last to those who had been working from early in the day. Imagine their irritation when it became clear that all who were hired, for however long or short a time, were to receive the same wages! How dare the landowner treat them that way! Had he no sense of fairness? After all it was his money they were fighting over. Was he not free to give it away to whom he chose? What was their problem, he asked. "Or are you envious because I am generous?" [Matthew 20:15].

I never grow tired of hearing such finely wrought tales. Each one contains layers of meaning no one person or generation can exhaust.

"Mother, he would say, "I want hearts to grow so generous that forgiveness will flow from them like rainwater rushing down every ravine into the sea. Without forgiveness of one another's offenses there is no hope for peace."

On another occasion Jesus chose to answer a question Peter posed not directly by means of exhortation but indirectly by relating a parable: "Lord, if another member of the church sins against me, how often should I forgive him? As many as seven times?" [Matthew 18:21]. Jesus gave a quick reply, "I say to you, not seven times but seventy-seven times" [Matthew 18:22]. To prove his point he told another brief but unforgettable story.

There was a king who wanted to settle accounts with his servant. He owed him a lot of money, and it was high time to pay his debt. The man, along with his wife and children, begged for a reprieve. Touched by their plea, the master not only agreed to wait, but on second thought, he decided to cancel the debt and let him go with no strings attached.

The master forgave the debt, but the story goes on to show just how difficult it is to forgive others as God has forgiven us. The now debtless servant goes out and finds a fellow servant who owed him some money. In a now familiar scene, the debtor begs for a reprieve. Only his plea is flatly refused. Not only is he humiliated; he is thrown by the unmerciful servant into debtor's prison. When the other servants saw what happened, despite the example of their master's generosity, they were distraught. They had no recourse but to report what they had seen. There was no escape. The servant who did not do for another what had been done so generously for him was rightly rebuked for lacking any semblance of compassion. He was more greedy than giving, more focused on his own gain than on the cruelty of this unforgiving act. Now it was his turn to go to jail. Then, Jesus said to Peter and the others, "So my heavenly Father will also do to everyone of you, if you do not forgive your brother or sister from your heart" [Matthew 18:35].

Once I saw Jesus sitting on the stoop in front of our house meticulously untying the knots of a string. As our eyes met, he saw the question in mine. "Mother," he said, "This is the way the Father unties the knots of humankind's mistakes."

I still have it, that piece of string. It reminds me of Jesus' words to Peter, when he called him the rock on which he would build his church, saying, "I will give you the keys of the kingdom of heaven, and whatever you bind on earth will be bound in heaven, and whatever you loose on earth will be loosed in heaven" [Matthew 16:19].

Jesus kept on untying those knots until that old gnarled string returned to its original free flowing state. He swung the string around in the air as if it were a soul loosened from the tight bonds of sin by forgiveness.

When I pass that unknotted string through my fingers, I pray that every soul in the world will heed the call to let go of all that holds them in prisons of their own making. I want to say to them, as Jesus might:

"Untie the knot of your failure. Destring those clumps of despair. Fan out your frustrations. Let grace untangle the thread of your destiny by releasing you from the net of your petty plans for revenge, your unholy desires. Let God be for you like a mighty eraser of forgiveness. Then go and do likewise for others. Bathe their wounds with the balm of your forgiveness. Pave a path whereon you and they can make a new start. Don't walk with your backs to one another but turn around and shake hands. Look up with renewed vigor to the stars of your mutual destiny. Change only takes three words, '*I forgive you.*' "

I find it impossible to hold this string without recalling also how much Jesus loved to fish. He was always restringing and testing his lines, ready in a flash to head for the sea when Joseph proposed an outing. He was happy as a boy could be when he brought home for supper a stringer heavy with their fresh catch. No wonder he called upon fishermen like Peter and Andrew to throw life lines to sinners, pulling as many as they could into the saving net of Jesus' teaching and never doubting God's will to offer them a new start.

Forgiveness is like that. It fishes out from our interiority what is impure in God's sight, what could make us spiritually, if not physically, diseased. It presents us to the Father in a state of grace. All he asks is that we pass this gift on to others by for giving them as we have been forgiven. This act of mercy blocks sin before it causes barnacles to grow on our heart. Until heaven comes to earth, we shall not cease to praise God for the gift of transformation through forgiveness.

TRANSFORMATION

How longing was my Son and Lord
to transform those
who mocked his word?
His sensitivity
did not deflate his pity
nor freeze the sea of mercy
pouring from his breaking heart.
Nothing could still
his loving will
to transform every
fiber of their being
even as they spilled his blood
drop by drop.

Mary, ask the Spirit,
to transform my heart,
bitter, smart,
sticking stubbornly
to the pains
heaped on me,
hopefully unwittingly.

Without prayer for their transformation
I cannot regain
peace in the midst of pain.
Relief and release come again
as I allow
your Son's holy power
to shower my soul,
rendering me whole,
arresting my running astray
from his transforming way.

CHAPTER NINE

Salvation

"And Lead Us Not into Temptation"

And lead us not into temptation . . . then what is the meaning of this phrase? It does not mean: do not allow us to come into temptation. It means: when we come into temptation, let us not be defeated by it.   —John Cassian

WHEN Jesus taught us to pray not to be put to the test or to be tried beyond our strength to endure, I remembered the conversations we had when he returned to Galilee after those forty long and lonely days in the desert.

No more would he be able to live in the sweet ambience of our hidden life in Nazareth. No more would people think of him as only a carpenter's son. His ministry had begun, and with it a series of events that would comprise the salvation history of the world.

In the desert his obedience was brought to the fullness of perfection. So profound were his experiences there that he almost hesitated to describe them in greater detail to me. He was in constant communion with the Father, oblivious, in the awe of contemplative bliss, to hunger and cold, heat and thirst.

He was at one with the entire cosmos, with every atom and molecule of creation. He was there where the world began and there where it would end.

As our saving Lord, his entire existence would have only one purpose: to say yes to the will of his Father. His life would be the living proof that God has loved us first [see 1 John 4:10]; that he sent his only Son into the world to save humankind from its sins—to seek the lost and bring them home.

"Mother, you can't imagine what a cosmic battle I fought. The devil used every possible means to force me to succumb. I would close my eyes to pray in silence and the racket of a thousand bazaars would descend upon the desert. Images from the most lascivious to the most luxurious would appear to dazzle me if I dared to open my eyes to behold a simple star.

"Every moment of concentration would be interrupted by caravans of distractions. Sleep, even a short doze to refresh me in my weariness, was impossible. Once I was surrounded by thousands of scorpions though they never stung me, by hoards of locusts though they never landed on my hair. I could neither sleep nor eat. The attacks never stopped. The heat of the devil's rage was more scorching than the sun by day; the cold of his hatred more freezing than the desert night. The wind was so fierce it tore the cloak from my back.

"Through it all I knelt and prayed. I raised my threadbare arms to the heavens and lay prostrate on the sand. All I did for forty days and nights was to stay in union with my Father's will in the innermost core of my being where no devilish force can penetrate."

My eyes never wavered from his gaunt face as he related these horrors. He knew that all during this time I was one with him in Spirit. Before he died, I decided to share with him what I went through: forty days and forty nights living only on bread and water, offering my life as a symbolic sacrifice for his well-being, praying without ceasing that the Father would shield him from the terrible ire of the Tempter.

"I, dearest Mother, ate nothing during those days. I neither could nor wanted to interrupt the depth of prayer that it was my destiny to reach and soon thereafter to teach. "When the time to leave the desert came, I realized how hungry I was. Now the devil thought he had the chance to undo the depth of detachment I had attained. "As always his first line of defense was to play on a person's pride commingled with the promise of pleasure. He said to me, 'If you are the Son of God, command this stone to become a loaf of bread' [Luke 4:3]. "

"Guided by the Spirit, I realized in an instant that I had to reply not directly, as an argument would have surely ensued, but indirectly by citing not my words but the truths in our teachings."

I repeat the passage to which he refers when I feel the hunger that comes from fasting: " 'One does not live by bread alone, but by every word that comes from the mouth of God' " [Matthew 4:4]. I agonize in my solitude for the children of God, those living now and in the ages to come. Many are the times they will be led into temptation. Who knows how many will fall? May God's words be written in their hearts and imprinted on their consciences.

"The Evil One does not give up so easily, Mother. The temptation to instant gratification had no hold on me, but the devil thought I could be dissuaded from my Father's plan if he could convince me of the importance of having my own base of power. He could not comprehend that the only real power lies in powerlessness."

He paused because the memory was painful and then said, "Somehow I found myself with him on a high plane from whence, in an instant, he conjured up before my tired and sleepless eyes an image of all the kingdoms of the world. I knew there was no denying that many lay under his power. It was no bluff to hear him say that he would give me all their authority and splendor, on one condition."

It horrified me to think that the devil would dare to propose to Jesus that he bow down and worship him. The boldness of evil knows no bounds. He would have Jesus break the first commandment that forbids idolatry of any sort.

I could almost picture my brave Son, so tired, so hungry, so fearless in the face of evil, again refusing to meet the devil on his ground and instead citing another passage from the holy book that would keep the soul safe in the face of temptation.

That is why he answered him, "It is written, 'Worship the Lord your God, and serve only him'" [Luke 4:8].

Still, this prince of lies would not leave my poor Son alone. Two rebuffs were insufficient. The devil does not give up that easily. This time he played on the human need to amass possessions, as if anything of this sort would be of interest to Jesus.

"Believe it or not, Mother, he led me to Jerusalem. Somehow I found myself on the highest point of the temple. Now he turned the tables on me and himself began to cite the scriptures. Once more he questioned my identity by saying: 'If you are the Son of God, throw yourself down from here, for it is written: "He will command his angels concerning you, to protect you", and "On their hands they will bear you up, so that you will not dash your foot against a stone" [Luke 4:10-11].

My Son's reply to this last attempt to usurp his power revealed the only true might: that of humility. He rebuked the Evil One by another perfect rebuttal, referring to the scriptures. "It also says, 'Do not put the Lord your God to the test'" [Luke 4:12].

Then the devil left him, hoping for a more opportune time to tempt Jesus to betray his call. Even in the hour of his greatest suffering, it never came. Perhaps out of sheer anger and frustration Satan never missed one occasion during Jesus' public ministry to try his patience—as when he had to chase the money changers from the temple [see John 2:12-17] or to rebuke the disciples for arguing foolishly as to who would be the greatest [see Luke 9:46-50].

In that devastating hour of Jesus' arrest and incarceration [see Luke 22:1-6], the devil proved that people could not only be tempted to do evil but through it to despoil their chances of salvation. Poor Judas is the person of whom I am thinking— not with anger or bitterness but with a mother's compassion. How could I not pray for sinners when they have such a for- midable foe as the devil seeking their destruction?

There was no group of people for whom Jesus felt more empathy in this regard than his own disciples. Though they loved him and willingly changed their lives for him, they were tempted by doubts and misgivings. All too often their worldly ideas seduced them to buy into rational arguments that suited their all too human assumptions about God's ways with us.

The conversation Jesus had that night with Nicodemus [see John 3:1-21] is a perfect example of what I mean. Here was a prestigious and knowledgeable person, a member of the Jewish ruling council, who had seen the signs and wonders my Son's ministry often required—so weak was the people's faith. He acknowledged what his eyes told him, but he was tempted to stop at disclosures of divine power instead of going deeper into their meaning.

Once again Jesus chose to take the indirect approach to lessen the impact of this temptation. He told Nicodemus that to really see, to fully comprehend with eyes of faith what was happening, he had to be born again.

The poor man was tempted to take these words literally. He could have chosen to walk away but instead he stayed with his teacher. The devil would have loved Nicodemus to dismiss Jesus' words as preposterous—but he did not do so. Instead he listened to what Jesus had to say about being born again of water and the spirit.

I know how much it pained Jesus that people saw and heard the wondrous things he did, though they did not themselves accept his testimony. They were led into temptation and consented to turn away. Nicodemus did not do so. He stayed, and that is why Jesus could say to him, "If I told you about earthly things and you do not believe, how can you believe if I tell you about heavenly things?" [John 3:12].

Jesus asked a lot of this teacher of Israel. It must have made him wince to hear Jesus speak of himself as the Son of Man. He must have been tempted again to close his ears and his heart to such a radical word. But he did not.

The devil loves to lead people to deny what their heart knows to be true, but they do not have to follow this path to destruction.

"I am there for them, Mother, from the moment they are tempted. One call and I will come to rescue them. That is why I so welcomed this meeting with Nicodemus. He gave me the chance to take him to a new place. I told him truths I had only shared with my closest followers. I wanted him to hear that '...God so loved the world that he gave his only Son, so that everyone who believes in him may not perish but may have eternal life'" [John 3:16].

"My Son," I replied, "sometimes I think that the greatest temptation with which people have to cope is their inability to believe that God loves them so much that he took the initiative to save them. The devil tempts them to assume the opposite— that their lives are hopeless, that their sins are unforgivable, that they do not deserve to be loved at all, let alone so outrageously that you would be sent, not to condemn the world but to redeem it. How hard it is for sinful people to believe that such love is possible!"

When the night was spent, Jesus and Nicodemus parted. The man needed time to reflect on all that he had heard, time to absorb the new found belief he felt. The light had come into the world, even though men continued to love the darkness and follow evil ways.

It is one thing to be tempted, another to consent. Jesus himself was tempted. It is the devil's role to test where people's hearts really are, but it is Jesus' role to give them the grace not to succumb.

Jesus never underestimated the dilemma in which Nicodemus must have found himself that night. He knew only too well from his own reading of the scriptures that everyone who does wicked things hates the light and does not come toward the light, so that his works might not be exposed [see John 3:20].

The way to overcome temptation is to live by the truth. All my life and especially now in my elder years, I have wondered why so many settle for the dark corridors of the devil's lies when God invites them to the sunlit meadows of the love that leads to their divine destiny.

Mere mortals though we are, God gives us an arsenal of defenses against the most devilish of temptations. In my own and Jesus' life, the surest defense has been obedience. Our yes to God is the barrier no evil can penetrate. It is offered freely without coercion. No temptation can still its course.

It must have been quite a contrast for Jesus to go from a conversation with one of Israel's renowned teachers to an encounter with an outcast like the Samaritan woman, but he had no problems with elitism or class consciousness. We are all God's children in his eyes. She was not only tempted to lie to him about her marital state; she actually did! But Jesus caught her before it was too late.

Though at that moment, she could say with some impunity, "I have no husband" [John 4:17], Jesus read what was in her mind's eye and revealed the fact that she had five husbands and was currently living with another man.

Imagine how ripe she was for the devil's seduction. But it was not Jesus' purpose to judge or condemn her. He wanted to

save her. And so, as was the case in a totally different context
with Nicodemus, their conversation continued. It was to her
that Jesus revealed a remarkable truth: "But the hour is coming, and is now here, when the true worshipers will worship
the Father in Spirit and truth; for the Father seeks such as
these to worship him" [John 4:23]. She herself would be one
of the worshipers sought by the Father, for she was willing to
change, anxious to grow, convinced by this meeting that she
was worthy to receive the grace of redemption.

Against any and all doubts the devil might have tried to
instill in her mind, she chose freely to listen and to believe
when Jesus confirmed her intuition that he was the Messiah,
the Christ, the Anointed One of God.

Jesus spent his public life striding across this battlefield of
belief and unbelief. Every believer was precious in his sight. I
often see their faces when I pray. I name their names—
Nicodemus, the Samaritan woman, the centurion, Zacchaeus,
Martha and Mary, Lazarus, Mary Magdalene. I remember as
a mighty bulwark against temptation, as witnesses to the
redemption, the nameless holy ones like the paralytic, the
blind beggar, the lepers, the widows, and those like the rich
young man who still struggle to choose: will it be God or
money [see Luke 18:18-25]?

Now, when the hungry come to my door and I feed them, as
I and Jesus and Joseph always did, I realize that in this simple act
there is a wealth of meaning. The devil wants us to forget the
ordinary as the place where God dwells. It is the Lord whom we
serve in those who hunger and thirst, who need hospitality and
clothing, who are lonely captives jailed by a lack of love.

One must not be tempted to seek God's face only on
mountain tops of transcendence. The danger of doing so
exposes people to the temptation of exclusivity or judgmental-
ism. Jesus wants us to see the Father everywhere. Abba's
omnipresence embraces us despite Satan's fury.

Normal tiredness overtakes me now. I want to rest and regain my strength. There are new battles to be fought on the way to eternal life, and I—mother of all souls in need of God's mercy–am at their side.

SALVATION

Mary, lovely servant of redemption
with your Lord,
praying over the millennia
unceasingly
that Gentile and Jew,
slave and free
will not lose deliverance
by eating the toxic fruit
of the forbidden tree
poisoning our taste
for the fruit of salvation
from the blood strained tree
on which Jesus died,
for us, crucified.

Help us to sense
God's saving marks
etched in our lonely hearts
longing to be whole,
imprints almost wiped out
by storms of temptation
trying to sweep away
your salvific animation.

No longer can you abide
by the simple village code
of your still abode
in Nazareth, surrounded as you are
by temples, vendors, carriages, streets,
by noise with no retreats
from theaters, public baths, soldiers, and bazaars.

As mother of humanity you sadly sense
how many are led
into temptation threatening salvation.
Do not leave us behind

crippled as we are
by the whirl of worldly agitation.
Restore in us the
power of salvation.

I hear you say to all:
my prayer speeds beyond the city wall.
I am enthralled by the sight
of sun, moon, stars,
still and bright
twinkling above my tired head,
when at last I go to bed.

I marvel at the universe
with every atom, molecule, and mutation,
unfolding within the salvation
of the mystery of creation.

How fondly Jesus cared,
how he himself shared
the demonic lure and charm
to help us calm
the satanic storm,
leaving behind
in heart and mind
the deadly worm of temptation.

Above and beyond it all,
my faith pauses in awe
before my Son's dwelling place
to be disclosed in all its grace
to you and me.

My love delights in the mystery of his will.
I smile with my Lord
so tender and bold,
bringing to his fold
those seeking salvation
from the madhouse of temptation.

CHAPTER TEN

Liberation

"But Deliver Us From Evil"

One certain conviction we have: that God is a powerful support since he grants his help to anyone who asks for it. Consequently, when we say: 'Deliver us from evil,' there is nothing else left for us to ask. Invoking the protection of God against evil means asking for everything we need.   —Cyprian of Carthage

THERE was something beautiful and something terrible in these few last words. They sent a tremor through the listeners gathered around Jesus. They felt that foreordained by his goodness was the assurance of their deliverance from the diseases of soul and body that used to seem invincible obstacles on their way to God. Now, through him, their liberation was at hand.

Still, even as we prayed with such hope, we felt a chill wind blowing across our faces on this otherwise warm and pleasant day. Evil was a formidable foe, and the Evil One was enraged beyond measure at the freedom from sin and death my Son promised to deliver to the people of God.

For a moment I caught his eye. Was it only a mother's intuition or something more that made me see written on his face the ecstasy of pure goodness commingled with the agony of the price he would have to pay for humankind's salvation?

There was no way to mitigate that from which we were praying to be delivered—all the hatred that divided human hearts and spawned devastation; all the greed that amassed earthly profits at the cost of losing one's soul; all the hypocrisy that judged others without repenting for one's own sins.

Jesus saw through every guise evil wears, making it all the more imperative that his message be obliterated. Many were the times when that sword Simeon predicted pierced my heart, for his prophecy proved to be true: that "this child is destined for the falling and rising of many in Israel, and to be a sign that will be opposed" [Luke 2:34].

Forecasts of that opposition already happened when our family hid away in Nazareth, but no event could have prepared us for what our son would have to endure, all because he was so good.

One day, believe it or not, he came home with swollen eyes and a bloody nose. The tears ran down my cheeks as I took him in my arms and tended his bruises. If only I could have helped him in the same way when he hung on the cross! Joseph ran in from the shop when he heard our voices and stood stunned in the doorway. He put his arms around both of us and asked, with the profound tenderness so characteristic of him, "Tell us, Son, how could such a thing have happened?"

As Jesus related how this beating occurred, I sensed the shocking contrast between good and evil. Seeing two boys spitting in each others' face, scratching, clawing, and calling names because they could not settle their differences, Jesus tried to step between them and stop the fight. He held them at arms' length while they struggled to hit one another. He said a few words which seemed to calm their anger, but no sooner had he stepped away than they turned viciously on him, pounding his face and yelling at him to mind his own business and drop his stupid requests for peace and reconciliation. Who did he think he was anyway to tell them what to do?

By now a gang had gathered and Jesus knew he was defenseless. He protected his head from further blows and remained silent. Unbeknown to them, he prayed, until one by one they walked away, uttering a last barrage of insults.

All three of us clung to one another. In our hearts we prayed for deliverance from the ancient diseases of racial and religious divisions that sparked the boys' fight in the first place. The evil that preys upon us does not expect to be prayed over. Yet this is what Jesus taught us to do.

Every line of his prayer was rooted in some experience of his life, and this last petition was no exception.

Countless are the evils that imprison the spirit. Jesus worked diligently, by teaching and example, to call attention to cowardice, avarice, and hypocrisy. He did not mince words when it came to showing what obedience to the law of love really meant. He warned that to follow him might itself divide brothers and sisters, parents and children, to such a degree, as he informed the Twelve, that ". . . you will be hated by all because of my name, but the one who endures to the end will be saved" [Matthew 10:22]. The aim of his and their teaching would be to do all in their power to prevent people from cutting themselves off from the law of love decreed by God.

Some of the most memorable words Jesus ever spoke in this regard were these:

"A disciple is not above his teacher, nor a slave above the master; it is enough for the disciple to be like the teacher, and the slave like the master. If they have called the master of the house Beelzebul, how much more will they malign those of his household! So have no fear of them; for nothing is covered up that will not become known. What I say to you in dark, tell in the light; and what you hear whispered, proclaim from the housetops" [Matthew 10:24-27].

Old as I am I feel the passion for truth surge through my limbs. If my voice were not so weakened by age, I would still make a fool of myself, climb to the roof, and shout with all the strength in me how good is God!

Jesus' message was never directed to a select few; he intended it to be heard by all. He sought to liberate human hearts from the chains shackling them to cowardice disguised as courage, to violence posing as love, to death masked as a way to life. His instructions to the community of faith have never been forgotten: "See, I am sending you like the sheep into the midst of wolves; so be wise as serpents and innocent as doves" [Matthew 10:16]

He was the lamb of God who would be slain for what he believed, for the truth he preached, but his ways were not then, nor will they ever be, forgotten. Cowards though the apostles themselves were tempted to be (look at what happened to Peter!), they had been equipped by Jesus with the tools they needed—not their own common sense only but the power of the Spirit, for "when they hand you over," he told them, "do not worry about how you are to speak or what you are to say; for what you are to say will be given to you at that time; for it is not you who speak, but the Spirit of your Father speaking through you" [Matthew 10:19-20].

As a mother who watched her Son pay the full price of deliverance from evil, I am comforted by the truth he proclaimed and indeed for which he gave his life—that we need not fear those "who kill the body but cannot kill the soul" [Matthew 10:28]. Rather we are to be afraid of the one who can destroy both soul and body in hell [see Matthew 10:28].

Cowards killed my Son, not brave, courageous, righteous people, but cowards. That is why they receive from me not condemnation (only God can judge them ultimately) but compassion.

There have been times in my life when I was afraid, too, like that night when I was about to give birth and there was no room for us at the inn [see Luke 2:7]. It did not matter to me, but would my newborn be safe in a stable? Then there was that dreadful time when we had to flee to Egypt [see Matthew 2:13-15] because Herod, out of sheer cowardice, slew so many innocents [see Matthew 2:16]. At heart-palpitating moments, as when Jesus was led away to prison, who would not be afraid? But his words were always there to comfort me: ". . .are not two sparrows sold for a penny? Yet not one of them will fall to the ground unperceived by your Father. And even the hairs of your head are all counted. So do not be afraid; you are of more value than many sparrows" [Matthew 10:29-31].

I thank my Son, my Risen Lord, for the many times he said, "Take heart, it is I; do not be afraid!" [Mark 6:50]. By these words, by his own bravery in the face of every evil known to man, he liberated his people from the debilitating effects of fear. He taught all who had the courage to listen a new way to live. To take up the cross is to banish cowardice and with it the most cowardly one of all, the prince of this world. Who would have expected evil's complete defeat to happen at the foot of a cross?

As much as Jesus sought to free his disciples from fear, he also did all he could to untie the gross knots of greed that caused so many to cling to wealth and worldly possessions as if in them resided the release they sought.

Ironically, the avaricious heart becomes possessed by its own possessions. Jesus could not bear it when people were so stingy they could not even part with a cup of water for a thirsty person [see Matthew 10:42]. Sadly for them, they did not know it was to him that this water was to be given.

He warned again and again about the entrapment riches, with no sense of right stewardship, posed to the soul. Perhaps his most powerful words in this regard were these: "No one can serve two masters; for a slave will either hate the one and love the other, or be devoted to the one and despise the other. You cannot serve God and wealth" [Matthew 6:24].

That's what I love so much about Joseph. He taught Jesus this truth by his own example. He worked faithfully everyday, providing for his family, but he never worried so much about his livelihood that he allowed money—the presence or lack of it—to diminish by so much as one ounce his faith in the providence of God nor did worldly cares ever interfere with his commitment to his family and to prayer.

He would take the boy Jesus out into the beautiful fields not far from our house and tell him, in words Jesus made his own: "Look at the birds of the air; they neither sow nor reap nor gather into barns, and yet your heavenly Father feeds them. Are you not of more value than they? And can any of you by worrying add a single hour to your span of life? And why do you worry about clothing? Consider the lilies of the field, how they grow; they neither toil nor spin, yet I tell you, even Solomon in all his glory was not clothed like one of these" [Matthew 6:26-29].

What accounts for greed, in Jesus' teaching, is not only the naive assumption that possessions are permanent. They are as passing as the dust I scoop up in my hand. All I have to do is open my fingers, and out it flows. No, the problem behind possessiveness is weakness of faith and, above all, lack of trust in the providence of God.

There were many times when Joseph and I wondered if we would have enough money to provide for our own but, above all, for Jesus' needs. Carpentry, with all the time and refinement Joseph put into it, produced a good living for us, but there was not much left over for the few extras we wanted our Son to have. He would smile and shake his head when we spoke of these things.

Years later he would tell the people, many as poor as we were, things he used to say to us: ". . . your heavenly Father knows that you need all these things. But strive first for the kingdom of God and his righteousness, and all these things will be given to you as well" [Matthew 6:32-33].

With his love surrounding us, we sought the way of holiness now summarized so simply in Jesus' prayer. It would be difficult even for me to recall all the parables he told warning peo-

ple about the dire consequences of choosing money and its
avaricious acquisition over the laws of good stewardship. He
told us to be generous, always ready to give even the little one
has to another in physical or spiritual need. Wealth is elusive,
God's way lasting.

Evil follows swiftly on the heels of avarice. That is why Jesus
spent so much time teaching people to recognize what hap-
pens when wealth is loved more than the way of the Lord.

Imagine how his words stung the avaricious ears of those
who were already plotting to destroy him. They hated to hear
stories of his like the one about the rich man and Lazarus [see
Luke 16:19-31]. These accounts turned the tables on their
assumptions about who is found most worthy in God's eyes.

Jesus was amazing in this regard. There wasn't one moment
I can remember when he did not share everything he had: one
bite out of a small cake and the rest went to someone hungri-
er. I could hardly keep the clothes on his back, so eager was he
to give them away to every shivering stranger.

No wonder these wily enemies of his—whose hypocrisy
aroused in my Son some of the most scathing criticism I ever
heard him utter—tried in every way to trip him up [see
Matthew 22:18].

One time it would involve picking and eating kernels of
corn on the Sabbath [see Matthew 12:1-8], as if he were not
its Lord. Another time entrapment would entail whether or
not to pay taxes to the emperor. That's when he asked these
hypocrites to hand him a coin. He turned the tables on them,
inquiring whose head was imprinted on it. They said "the
emperor's," to which he replied in simple words they despised:
"Give . . . to the emperor the things that are the emperor's, and
to God the things that are God's" [Matthew 22:21].

Hypocrisy was an evil Jesus could not countenance, especially in people like the scribes and the pharisees who were
supposed to be exemplary teachers of the law. Were they or

were they not witnesses to the liberation promised when we obey the Great Commandment to love God with our whole heart and soul and mind and to love our neighbor as we love ourselves [see Matthew 22:36- 40].

Hypocrisy meant telling people to observe the greatest to the least commandment, lest they incur God's wrath, and then not doing so oneself. It meant parading one's spiritual importance like proud peacocks in public and doing the opposite in private. It was expecting to be called a teacher with absolutely no intention to be a learner. It was forgetting the truth that "all who exalt themselves will be humbled, and all who humble themselves will be exalted" [Matthew 23:12].

Woe to frauds who dared to decide on their own who would enter into or be shut out of God's reign; who turned converts into devils like themselves; who pretended they knew how and where to direct seekers but who themselves were blind guides and fools of the worst sort, unable to distinguish, as Jesus said, between "the gold or the sanctuary that has made the gold sacred" [Matthew 23:17].

That Son of mine certainly had a way with words! No wonder these hypocrites were determined to silence him forever, not realizing that his words would never pass away [see Matthew 24:35].

They did not want to hear his "woes" to them—these blind guides who strained out the gnat and swallowed the camel! [see Matthew 23:24]; who cleansed "the outside of the cup and of the plate, but inside they are full of greed and self-indulgence" [Matthew 23:25]; who were "like whitewashed tombs, which on the outside look beautiful, but inside they are full of the bones of the dead and all kinds of filth" [Matthew 23:27].

Jesus' conclusion must have sealed their determination to kill him. He felt the sword pierce my heart as this battle between good and evil raged, but he could not stand aside while lies were told that left people vulnerable to demonic seduction with little hope of deliverance.

Shortly before his arrest, he held my tearful face in his tender hands and said, "Mother, you would have done the same." It was my Son after all who could not bear anymore than I the fact that on the outside you appear righteous, but inside you are filled with hypocrisy and evildoing [see Matthew 23:28].

Given these sayings, it was only a matter of time before my brave and holy Child would himself be delivered into evil hands—not to be defeated, as they predicted, but to break through death's barrier and bring new life to the world. He was the temple destroyed who in three days would rise again.

I have seen, as he predicted, the mushrooming of false messiahs and prophets, performing signs and wonders [see Matthew 24:24], hypocritically misleading the gullible who run from deserts to amphitheaters seeking salvation when Jesus has already opened the door [see Matthew 24:33].

When I glance at the portal of the little house where I live in Ephesus, it is as if he always stands there in light as radiant as the sun, comforting me with these precious memories of his earthly ministry. Soon enough I shall arrive at heaven's door, but for now it is enough to see the stars above my head, forming a great canopy alight with my Creator's love.

How swiftly these adoring words form on my lips. I rise with arms stretched heavenward, swept up in a motion that matches the music of the spheres, praising God and saying, as our holy family so often did, "For thine is the kingdom and the power and the glory, now and forever, Amen!"

LIBERATION

Lady of all nations, rejoice,
in this strange and foreign land
deliverance is close at hand.
Your soul overflows with commiseration
pining for liberation
of all humanity,
compassion replacing condemnation,
delivery from the tragedy
of dissonance, disharmony.

In the depths of your memory
reverberates the agony
you suffered with your Child
when lifted up above wild
insults pitched at him from every side
by enemies in a crowd,
vicious, mean, and loud.

May his agony
grant all nations liberty
from captivity to
expediency.

Destroy the tombstones
of feigned correctness
that cover the waywardness
of lifeless hearts.
End racial and religious strife,
the cruel divide
separating mother, child, husband, wife,
friend and foe,
each nation's deepening woe.

Heal that faint-heartedness
imprisoning our spirit.
Let us be and do our best
in the fellowship of the elect,
faith-filled not faint-hearted,
following Jesus
honest and erect,
ready to fight the good fight
until we go gently into the night
of final liberation.

CONCLUSION

The "Our Father" prayer contains all the fullness of perfection, inasmuch as the Lord himself has given it to us, both as a model and also as a precept. Those who are familiar with this prayer are raised by it to a very lofty condition, namely that 'prayer of fire' which very few know by direct experience and which it is impossible to describe.

The 'prayer of fire' transcends all human feeling. There are no longer sounds of the voice nor movements of the tongue nor articulated words. The soul is completely imbued with divine light. Human language, always inadequate, is no use any more. But in the soul is a spring bubbling over, and prayer gushing out from it leaps up to God. The soul expresses in a single instant many things which could only be described or remembered with difficulty when it has returned to its normal condition.

Our Lord has traced an outline of this mystical state in this formula, the 'Our Father' that contains various supplications, and also in the hours he spent alone on the mountain side, and in the silent prayer of his agony in the moment when he even sweated blood through the unique intensity of his unity with the Father.

—John Cassian

THIS book has been a meditation on the Lord's Prayer through the eyes of Mary. It is offered to you not as a learned treatise but as a imaginative treatment of ancient truths challenging you to take a second look at your spirituality.

Is your prayer life sufficiently in touch with everydayness— with the Nazareths in which you live?

97

Do you see the connection between Holy Scripture and the script a Mighty Hand pens for you daily?

Do you sense that turning to God for guidance is not a once and for all point of conversion but saying yes, "Thy will not mine be done," as a matter of course?

By praying the Lord's Prayer in the company of his mother, we find a freshness in these familiar words that makes us want to pray the prayer not routinely but contemplatively. In this matter we are in good company. According to the ancient Church Father Tertullian, the Lord's Prayer "is truly a summary of the whole gospel."[1] Saint Thomas Aquinas calls it "the most perfect of prayers," one that teaches us not only "to ask for things, but also in what order we should desire them."[2]

This prayer was the source of much commentary in the early church. One of the best examples is by Saint Cyprian of Carthage (200-258), whose writings were influenced by Tertullian. He calls the Our Father "a friendly and intimate prayer," one in which we beseech God in his own words, assured that "the prayer of Christ [will] ascend to his ears."[3]

The Cappodocian Father, Saint Gregory of Nyssa (335-394), wrote an entire book on the Lord's Prayer and the Beatitudes.[4] In the *Catechism of the Catholic Church*, Saint Gregory is cited as saying, "We must contemplate the beauty of the Father without ceasing and adorn our own souls accordingly."[5] He stands in the tradition of many saints and mystics who believe these salutations and petitions are an opening to that prayer without ceasing of which scripture speaks [see 1 Thessalonians 5:16-18].

Origen wrote of the Lord's Prayer in his *Exhortation to Martyrdom* in the third century; Augustine devoted many sermons to its petitions in the fourth century. The prayer permeated the undivided church of the east and the west, leading Saint Maximus the Confessor (580-662) to say in his commentary that "there exists but one happiness, a communion of life with the word, the loss of which is an endless punishment that goes on for all eternity."[6] The early Fathers minced no words when it came to the union of our will with God's.

In the medieval era, catechetical instructions were often given as meditations on the scriptures and few passages were as popular as those on the Lord's Prayer. Saint Thomas Aquinas (1224-1274) made it the basis for his own teaching in the thirteenth century as did Saint Teresa of Avila (1515-1582) in the sixteenth. Starting with Chapter 27 in her book, *The Way of Perfection* until its ending in Chapter 42, she discusses each petition of the prayer as itself an introduction on how to move with grace from vocal to mental to contemplative prayer and union with God. Saint Teresa's commentary is unique because she writes much of it in the form of her own style of praying the Our Father, interspersed with excellent counsels to her sisters on techniques that move prayer from the lips, into the mind, and through the heart.

At the start of her teaching she makes this inquiry of her sisters: "Does it seem right to you now that even though we recite these first words vocally we should fail to let our intellects understand and our hearts break in pieces at seeing such love?"[7] She tells her sisters in so many words to become great lovers of God as Jesus wished—not to be shy but to cast themselves into his waiting arms, to adore God with every fiber of their being, not with a weak faith vulnerable to changing tides but with a faith as strong as the walls surrounding Avila.

It is customary for Teresa to cite other masters on prayer, none of whom was more important to her than Saint Augustine. Reading his own *Confessions* was of great influence at the time of her conversion.[8] What happened to him she hopes will happen to her sisters as they bind their lips, minds, and hearts to these words of Jesus. For is it not as true for them, as it was for us, that we seek God in many places and ultimately find him within ourselves? That is why the journey to prayer must be personalized. No technique or rule is meant to cover all cases. We pray to God through the aperture of our own unique-communal life call.

Saint Teresa shows great respect for her sisters in this regard, reminding them that "However softly we speak, he is near enough to hear us."[9] In the course of these instructions, the saint shows a remarkable balance between informational and formational theology. She knows well the faith tradition that sustains her, but she also shows great finesse in bringing it home to the here and now formative needs of her sisters, in short, to their everyday character formation in Christ. In the process of commenting line by line on the Our Father, she answers their questions about the difference between true and false humility, petitionary prayers and recollection, simple union and consummate communion, the highest state of mystical marriage. She knows from prior experience of living under a mitigated rule, compared to being in a reformed community, what it means to walk from the Calvary of undiluted obedience to Christ Crucified to the glory of Easter morn. What makes her teaching so formative is its specificity.

This Doctor of the Church goes into details more speculative theologians may be inclined to gloss over. For example, in trying to help her novices grow in the art of recollection, she advises them when they pray to keep their eyes closed. Then she explains why this is a praiseworthy custom.

> . . .in the beginning the body causes difficulty because it claims its rights without realizing that it is cutting off its own head by not surrendering. If we make the effort, practice this recollection for some days, and get used to it, the gain will be clearly seen; we will understand, when beginning to pray, that the bees are approaching and entering the beehive to make honey.[10]

While Teresa, along with holy men like Saint John of the Cross and Saint Ignatius of Loyola, was engaged in what Church history would come to see in the sixteenth century as the Counter-Reformation, Martin Luther was making his mark as a leading figure in the Protestant Reformation. In the "Large Catechism" in the Book of Concord he reminds people that prayer is not a choice but a command, not a whim of the will but a solemn duty. He says that when we call upon our heavenly Father prayer comes spontaneously, "as it should, and we shall not need to be taught how to prepare for it or how to generate devotion."[11] As to the petitions of the Lord's Prayer, he believes that they comprehend "all the needs that continually beset us, each one so great that it should impel us to keep praying for it all our lives."[12]

Luther comments on each petition of the Lord's Prayer, finding in all of them divine directives that lead to holiness of life, reformation of all that separates us from our eternal heritage, protection from the wiles of the world, the flesh, and the devil. He counsels us to pray with confidence, with a kind of holy boldness—not to fear asking God for what we need and expecting in some providential way to receive it. "We must pray," he says, "that [God's] will be done among us, without hindrance, in spite of their [the devils'] fury, so that they may accomplish nothing and we may remain steadfast in the face of all violence and persecution, submitting to the will of God."[13]

Luther's conclusion is one we might all take to heart. He notes with the characteristic courage of his convictions, "But the efficacy of prayer consists in our learning also to say 'Amen' to it—that is, not to doubt that our prayer is surely heard and will be granted. . .where such faith is wanting, there can be no true prayer."[14]

Closer to our own time, many outstanding authors have been drawn to deepen their understanding and practice of the life of prayer through reflection on the Our Father.

Romano Guardini (1885-1968) was an Italian-born German priest whose books on the life of the spirit were acclaimed worldwide, answering people's thirst for God even as they sought to find faith in a time of radical transition in church and society. No amount of skepticism or the doubt arising from all too ample evidence of dehumanization could bend his faith. God used him in a trying time to guide and inspire especially the postwar German Catholic Youth Movement.

One of his best loved books, titled simply *The Lord's Prayer*, voices his certainty that the mystery of God's love remains with us in the darkest hour. He says we must never let an exaggerated sense of individual consciousness replace our consciousness of God as the heart and soul of our existence. His warning then makes even more sense now as narcissism and self-preoccupation nearly cancel the wisdom that comes through the hardships of living. Guardini observes:

> It would indeed be easier to let the heart follow its inclination; to think vaguely of the heavenly Father as of the far-flung heaven spanning a summer landscape, or to conjure up from somewhere the feeling of being safe and cherished. But the Lord's Prayer warns us: Beware! It is not by integration with the natural world that you are God's child, but by grace and faith.[15]

One woman whose acumen in this regard ought not to surprise us is the French mystic and intellectual Simone Weil (1909-1943). She is a person who probed the depths of human affliction and who saw in adversity an avenue to the stars. In pursuing the question of God, she could not separate herself from the question of divine forgiveness—freely offered, awesomely received—and the demand it makes upon us to forgive others as God has forgiven us. We learn from her writings and from various biographical accounts that after a visit to Assisi a few years before her untimely death from malnutrition (she maintained during the war that her rations of food should not exceed that of her compatriots who had not been able to escape the Nazi occupation of France), she began to recite the Lord's Prayer on a daily basis—not routinely, with the lips only, but with conviction, wholeheartedly. How faithful Simone was to her own words! "If we accept death completely, we can ask God to make us live again, purified from the evil in us. For to ask him to forgive us our debts is to ask him to wipe out the evil in us. Pardon is purification."[16]

Another soul formed, reformed, and transformed by the war experience was Alfred Delp (1907-1945), a Jesuit priest living in Nazi Germany, whose protest of the atrocities he witnessed around him led to his own imprisonment and death. It was at this low ebb of his life, when the walls of earthly existence were closing in upon him, that he experienced, perhaps for the first time, what the words of the Lord's Prayer really meant:

> When things are going well we let these words pass over us negligently, thinking very little about them, as if they really did not apply to us at all. And then all of a sudden the sky becomes overcast. . .take this journey of mine up the perilous face of my cliff . . . How is it that conditions suddenly get distorted, their balance disturbed and their threads twisted and entangled producing a pattern far from our intention and quite beyond our power to unravel? No one can escape the hour of temptation . . . If only I can manage to keep a hold on this perilous perch and not faint and let go.[17]

From this sampling of texts on the prayer of Jesus from ancient to medieval to modern times, one is left with the impression its secrets will never fully be unlocked. We have prayed this prayer through the imaginative sensibility of Mary to refresh our appreciation of its vitality and originality. These are words of wisdom whose efficacy only becomes richer with each passing day. No wonder so many pass from earth to heaven with this divine text on their lips. Every reiteration, rephrasing, or rewriting of it only seems to prove the point supported by our faith and formation tradition that the Lord's Prayer is a synopsis of the whole gospel, "the distillation of the substance of the good news."[18]

THE LAST WORD

"Our Father"
Your gentle word is present everywhere,
your holy name is etched into our heart.
we long to see you face to face,
to say yes to your wisdom with our whole being,
not only here and now
but for an eternity of affirmation.

Please give us day by day what we need to grow

physically

emotionally

functionally

spiritually.

Grant us the grace of sensing that you are there
to steady our steps when we fall,
on one condition: that we extend the same courtesy to others.

Save us from sly temptations to
cowardice
greediness
hypocrisy
despair
unkindness
envy, lust, and rage.

Purify that in us which still reeks
of pride and possessiveness,
of narcissism and self-preoccupation.

Deliver us from chasms of sin,
for you alone can save us,
You alone are majesty, glory, peace, and joy.
Amen! Alleluia! Amen!

END NOTES

[1] As cited in *The Catechism of the Catholic Church* (Mahwah, New Jersey: Paulist Press), Paragraph 2761.

[2] Ibid, Paragraph 2763.

[3] As cited in Nicholas Ayo, *The Lord's Prayer: A Survey Theological and Literary* (Notre Dame, Indiana: University of Notre Dame Press), 1992, p. 118.

[4] See St. *Gregory of Nyssa: The Lord's Prayer. The Beatitudes,* Translated and and annotated by Hilda C. Graef (Westminster, Maryland: Newman Press), 1954.

[5] *Catechism of the Catholic Church,* Paragraph 2784.

[6] See Nicholas Ayo, *The Lord's Prayer,* p. 136.

[7] St. Teresa of Avila, *The Way of Perfection,* in *The Collected Works of St. Teresa of Avila,* Volume Two, Translated by Kiernan Kavanaugh, O.C.D., and Otilio Rodriquez, OC.D. (Washington, D.C.: Institute of Carmelite Studies), 1980, 27:5, p. 139.

[8] See St. *Teresa of Avila, The Book of Her Life,* in *The Collected Works of St. Teresa of Avila,* Volume One, Translated by Kiernan Kavanaugh, O.C.D., and Otilis Rodriquez, O.C.D. (Washington, D.C.: Institute of Carmelite Studies), 1976.

[9] *The Way of Perfection,* 28:2, p. 140.

[10] Ibid, 28:7, p. 143.

[11] Martin Luther, "Large Catechism," in *The Book of Concord,* Translated and edited by Theodore G. Tappert (Philadelphia, Pennsylvania: Fortress Press), 1959, p. 424.

[12]   Ibid, p. 425.

[13]   Ibid, p. 429.

[14]   Ibid, p. 436.

[15]   Romano Guardini, *The Lord's Prayer*, (Manchester, New Hampshire: Sophia Institute Press), 1996, p. 23. This is a reprint of the 1932 original published in Germany under the title *Das Gebet des Herrn.*

[16]   Nicholas Ayo, *The Lord's Prayer*, pp. 166-167.

[17]   Ibid, p. 175.

[18]   Ibid, p. 6.

BIBLIOGRAPHY

Ayo, Nicholas. *The Lord's Prayer.* Notre Dame: University of Notre Dame Press, 1992.

Barclay, William. *The Beatitudes and the Lord's Prayer for Every Man.* New York: Harper and Row, 1968.

_____. *The Plain Man Looks at the Lord's Prayer.* Glasgow: Collins, 1964.

Barth, Karl. *Prayer.* Philadelphia: Westminster, 1985.

Becker, Karl and Marie Peter, Eds. *Our Father: A Handbook for Meditation.* Chicago: Regnery, 1956.

Berrigan, Daniel. *The Words Our Savior Gave Us.* Springfield, IL: Templegate, 1978.

Berthold, George Charles. *Selected Writings of Maximum Confessor,* New York: Paulist, 1985, pp. 107-112. The book is part of the Paulist series Classics of Western Spirituality.

Boff, Leonardo. *The Lord's Prayer: The Prayer of Integral Liberation.* Maryknoll, NY: Orbis, 1983.

Cartwright, Colbert S. *The Lord's Prayer Comes Alive.* St. Louis: Bethany Press, 1973.

Chase, Frederick H. *The Lord's Prayer in the Early Church.* Cambridge: Cambridge University Press, 1891; reprint, Nendeln, Liechtenstein: Kraus, 1967.

Claudel, Paul. *Lord, Teach Us to Pray.* New York: Longmans & Green, 1948.

Collins, Joseph B. *The Catechetical Instructions of St. Thomas Aquinas.* New York: Joseph F. Wagner, 1939, pp. 149-154.

Crosby, Michael. *Thy Will be Done: Praying the Our Father as Subversive Activity.* Maryknoll, NY: Orbis, 1977.

Davidson, John A. *The Lord's Prayer.* New York: World Publishing, 1970.

Defeeari, Roy. "About the Lord's Prayer," in *Saint Cyprian Treatises.* New York: Fathers of the Church, Inc. 1958, pp. 127-136.

Delp, Alfred. *The Prison Meditations of Father Alfred Delp.* New York: Herder and Herder, 1963.

Dods, Marcus. *The Prayer That Teaches Us to Pray.* New Canaan, CT: Keats Publishing, 1980.

Ebeling, Gerhard. *The Lord's Prayer in Today's World.* London: S.C.M. Press, 1966.

Evely, Louis. *We Dare to Say Our Father.* New York: Herder & Herder, 1965.

Graef, Hilda C. *St. Gregory of Nyssa: The Lord's Prayer: The Beatitudes.* Westminster, Maryland: Newman Press, 1954, pp. 45-50. This book is volume 18 of the Ancient Christian Writers series. Copyright © Paulist Press.

Harner, Philip. *Understanding the Lord's Prayer.* Philadelphia: Fortress Press, 1975.

Jeremias, Joachim. *The Lord's Prayer.* Philadelphia: Fortress Press, 1964.

Kavanagh, Denis J. *Saint Augustine: Commentary on the Lord's Sermon on the Mount with Seventeen Related Sermons.* New York: Fathers of the Church, 1951, p.143.

Keller, Weldon Phillip. *A Layman Looks at the Lord's Prayer.* Chicago: Moody Press, 1976.

LaVerdiere, Eugene. *When We Pray: Meditations on the Lord's Prayer.* Notre Dame, IN: Ave Maria Press, 1983.

Maritain, Raïssa. *Notes on the Lord's Prayer.* New York: P. J. Kenedy, 1964.

Muto, Susan. *Blessings that Make Us Be: A Formative Approach to Living the Beatitudes.* New York: Crossroad; Reprinted Petersham, MA: St. Bede's, 1982.

_____. *John of the Cross for Today: The Ascent.* Pittsburgh, PA: Epiphany Books, 1998.

_____. *John of the Cross for Today: The Dark Night.* Pittsburgh, PA: Epiphany Books, 2000.

_____. *Meditation in Motion.* New York: Doubleday, 1986.

_____. *Pathways of Spiritual Living.* New York: Doubleday; Reprinted Petersham, MA: St. Bede's Publications, 1988.

_____. *A Practical Guide to Spiritual Reading.* Petersham, MA: St. Bede's Publications, 1994.

_____ and Adrian van Kaam. *Divine Guidance: Seeking to Find and Follow the Will of God.* Pittsburgh, PA: Epiphany Books, 1994.

_____ and Adrian van Kaam. *The Commandments: Ten Ways to a Happy Life and a Healthy Soul.* Ann Arbor: Servant Publications, 1996.

O'Meara, John J. *Origen: Prayer: Exhortation to Martyrdom,* Westminster, Maryland: Newman Press, 1954, pp. 92-105. This book is volume 19 of the Ancient Christian Writers series.

Sheed, Francis. *The Lord's Prayer: The Prayer of Jesus.* New York: Seabury, 1975.

Thielicke, Helmut. *Our Heavenly Father: Sermons on the Lord's Prayer.* New York: Harper & Row, 1960.

Trueblood, Elton. *The Lord's Prayers.* New York: Harper & Row, 1965.

Underhill, Evelyn. *Abba: Meditations Based on the Lord's Prayer.* London: Longmans & Green, 1940.

van Kaam, Adrian. *Looking for Jesus*. Denville: Dimension Books, Inc., 1978.

_____. *Spirituality and the Gentle Life*. Pittsburgh: Epiphany Books, 1994.

_____. *The Tender Farewell of Jesus*. Hyde Park: New City Press, 1996.

_____. *The Woman at the Well*. Pittsburgh: Epiphany Books, 1993.

van Kaam, Adrian and Susan Muto. *Practicing the Prayer of Presence*. Totowa, NJ: Resurrection Press, 1993.

_____ and Susan Muto. *The Power of Appreciation: A New Approach to Personal and Relational Healing*. Pittsburgh, PA: Epiphany Books, 1999.

Weil, Simone. *Waiting for God*. New York: Putnam, 1951.

Books by Susan Muto

Approaching the Sacred: An Introduction to Spiritual Reading
Blessings That Make Us Be: A Formative Approach to Living the Beatitudes
Caring for the Caregiver
Catholic Spirituality from A to Z: An Inspirational Dictionary
Celebrating the Single Life
Dear Master: Letters on Spiritual Direction Inspired by Saint John of the Cross,
A Companion to *The Living Flame of Love*
John of the Cross for Today: The Ascent
John of the Cross for Today: The Dark Night
The Journey Homeward
Late Have I Loved Thee: The Recovery of Intimacy
Meditation in Motion
Pathways of Spiritual Living
A Practical Guide to Spiritual Reading
Renewed at Each Awakening
Steps Along the Way
Womanspirit: Reclaiming the Deep Feminine in our Human Spirituality
Words of Wisdom for Our World: The Precautions and Counsels
of St. John of the Cross

With Adrian van Kaam

Aging Gracefully
Am I Living A Spiritual Life?
The Commandments: Ten Ways to a Happy Life and a Healthy Soul
Commitment: Key to Christian Maturity
Divine Guidance: Seeking to Find and Follow the Will of God
The Emergent Self
Epiphany Manual on the Art and Discipline of Formation-in-Common
Formation Guide To Becoming Spiritually Mature
Harnessing Stress: A Spiritual Quest
Healthy and Holy Under Stress: A Royal Road to Wise Living
The Participant Self
The Power of Appreciation: A New Approach to Personal and Relational Healing
Practicing the Prayer of Presence
Readings from A to Z: The Poetry of Epiphany
Songs for Every Season
Stress and the Search for Happiness: A New Challenge for Christian Spirituality
Tell Me Who I Am
The Woman's Guide to the Catechism of the Catholic Church

111

Additional Titles Published by Resurrection Press, a Catholic Book Publishing Imprint

A Rachel Rosary *Larry Kupferman*	$4.50
Blessings All Around *Dolores Leckey*	$8.95
Catholic Is Wonderful *Mitch Finley*	$4.95
Come, Celebrate Jesus! *Francis X. Gaeta*	$4.95
Days of Intense Emotion *Keeler/Moses*	$12.95
From Holy Hour to Happy Hour *Francis X. Gaeta*	$7.95
Healing through the Mass *Robert DeGrandis, SSJ*	$9.95
Our Grounds for Hope *Fulton J. Sheen*	$7.95
The Healing Rosary *Mike D.*	$5.95
Healing Your Grief *Ruthann Williams, OP*	$7.95
Heart Peace *Adolfo Quezada*	$9.95
Life, Love and Laughter *Jim Vlaun*	$7.95
Living Each Day by the Power of Faith *Barbara Ryan*	$8.95
The Joy of Being a Catechist *Gloria Durka*	$4.95
The Joy of Being a Eucharistic Minister *Mitch Finley*	$5.95
The Joy of Being a Lector *Mitch Finley*	$5.95
The Joy of Being an Usher *Gretchen Hailer, RSHM*	$5.95
The Joy of Marriage Preparation *McDonough/Marinelli*	$5.95
The Joy of Music Ministry *J.M. Talbot*	$6.95
The Joy of Preaching *Rod Damico*	$6.95
The Joy of Teaching *Joanmarie Smith*	$5.95
Lights in the Darkness *Ave Clark, O.P.*	$8.95
Loving Yourself for God's Sake *Adolfo Quezada*	$5.95
Mother Teresa *Eugene Palumbo, S.D.B.*	$5.95
Personally Speaking *Jim Lisante*	$8.95
Practicing the Prayer of Presence *van Kaam/Muto*	$8.95
Prayers from a Seasoned Heart *Joanne Decker*	$8.95
5-Minute Miracles *Linda Schubert*	$4.95
Season of New Beginnings *Mitch Finley*	$4.95
Season of Promises *Mitch Finley*	$4.95
Soup Pot *Ethel Pochocki*	$8.95
Stay with Us *John Mullin, SJ*	$3.95
Surprising Mary *Mitch Finley*	$7.95
What He Did for Love *Francis X. Gaeta*	$5.95
You Are My Beloved *Mitch Finley*	$10.95
Your Sacred Story *Robert Lauder*	$6.95

For a free catalog call 1-800-892-6657